PROVERBS

A SELF-STUDY GUIDE

Irving L. Jensen

MOODY PRESS

CHICAGO

Cover photo: Solomon's Pools at Jerusalem

ISBN: 0-8024-4471-7

5 7 9 10 8 6 4

Printed in the United States of America

Contents

Introduction

The Bible was written primarily to show sinful man how he can be transformed and restored to fellowship with God. This doctrine of salvation pervades all of Scripture and is especially prominent in certain books (e.g., Romans). The Bible was also written to show the transformed sinner how to live a life pleasing to God now that he is saved. This instruction is to be found throughout Scripture, but it is the *main* theme of particular Bible books. Proverbs is one of these.

Most Christians are acquainted with the book of Proverbs, but not many have ever read or studied its entire text. Here is a book that is as important as it is practical. It surely was intended by God to make an impact on the lives of all His children.

God knows all. That is why His Book, the Bible, should be received as true doctrine and true instruction. When a Christian reads in Proverbs about a path to be avoided, he should heed the warning and stay away from such a path. He does not *have* to learn the hard way by tasting the bitter fruits of sinful acts. He should learn God's way by the instruction of His Word. And when Proverbs describes a path to be trodden, that is where the believer should be walking. Such is the kind of help the book offers. As you begin your study of Proverbs, let your goal be that expressed in the testimony of David:

> By the word of Thy lips
> I have kept from the paths of the violent.
> My steps have held fast to Thy paths.
> My feet have not slipped.
> Psalm 17:4-5, NASB*

*New American Standard Bible.

4

Suggestions for Study

1. The first two lessons of this manual are "starter" lessons, devoted to background and survey. These will help you get the *feel* of the book of Proverbs.

2. The remaining lessons are your guides in analyzing the text of Proverbs's thirty-one chapters. Each of these lessons is broken down into six parts:

(a) *Preparation for study.* Suggestions given here will help you get that *initial* momentum for studying the passage.

(b) *Analysis.* This is the core of your study. The manual's contribution is mainly through "search" questions and directions.

(c) *Notes.* These notes are usually facts or interpretations not available from the Bible passage itself.

(d) *For Thought and Discussion.* Application of the Bible text is the main appeal here. If you are studying in a group, open discussion of the subjects will be profitable.

(e) *Further Study.* Subjects for extended studies beyond the manual's lesson are suggested here. Continuity in the lesson is not lost if these studies are bypassed.

(f) *Words to Ponder.* A phrase of the Bible text set off by itself can often be most revealing. This pause at the end of each lesson is a reminder of the importance of *meditation* on God's holy Word.

3. You may want to study some lessons in two or more parts because of the length of the passage involved.

4. There are three basic tools for study: a good Bible text, paper, and pencil.

5. Develop personal study habits that are suited to your own abilities and inclinations. The following elements are basic to effective study, whatever method is used:

(a) Schedule. Set aside time; set aside a regular time.

(b) Desire. Guard this with all your strength.

(c) Methodicalness. Avoid dabbling in a haphazard fashion; learn and apply different methods suggested.

(d) Observation. See for yourself *what* the Bible says and *how* it says it.

(e) Recording. Keep your pencil busy. This is one of the main emphases of this self-study series.

(f) Dependence. Look to the Spirit's enlightenment as you interpret the biblical text.

6. The following outside helps will facilitate your study:

(a) One or two good modern Bible versions. Compare other translations with the Bible text given. (The King James version is the version quoted throughout this manual, unless otherwise specified.)

(b) A Bible dictionary or Bible encyclopedia. This is especially helpful for obtaining more information on people and places.

(c) A commentary. *The Wycliffe Bible Commentary* is recommended as a companion to these self-study guides.

Suggestions for Teachers of Bible Classes

1. Make clear to the members of the class what you want them to do in preparation for the next meeting. Encourage them to write out answers to all questions of the manual and jot down observations on charts when these are called for.

2. Emphasize the importance of spending time reading the Bible text itself. One cannot interpret the Bible correctly if he does not read the text correctly.

3. Stimulate discussion during the class meeting. Encourage everyone to participate. Some can do more; some can do less; but all can do something. You as leader should be prepared to ask the right questions to draw out of the class an ongoing discussion.

4. Encourage the members to ask questions about difficult proverbs. Recognize problem passages in the Bible when they appear. Use these occasions to emphasize the maxim of interpretation that *whatever is essential is clear.*

5. If possible, reproduce the charts of the manual on a chalkboard or on a screen using an overhead projector. Refer to the charts from time to time in the course of your class discussion. Remember the importance of the "eye gate" for teaching.

6. Devote the last part of your meeting to sharing the spiritual lessons taught by the Scripture passage. This should be the climax of the class hour.

Lesson 1
Background of the Book of Proverbs

God inspired the writing of Proverbs partly as an antidote to the spiritual apostasy of His people Israel. Like all Scripture, the book of Proverbs arose out of an immediate, local setting, involving people and their relationships to each other and to God. An understanding of the setting and characteristics of this twentieth book of the Bible will greatly enhance our study of its text. This in turn will make it easier for us to apply Proverbs to our lives. Such is the scope of this opening lesson.

I. TITLE

The common title of the book is "Proverbs," from the opening phrase, "The proverbs of Solomon," in 1:1. The Hebrew word for "proverb," *mashal*, comes from a root meaning "to be like," or "to represent." This is appropriate, since most proverbs use comparison to teach their truths. (An example: "He that hath no rule over his own spirit is like a city that is broken down, and without walls," 25:28.) Proverbs are terse maxims about conduct and character, primarily in the spiritual, moral, and social realms. When brought together in an anthology such as the book of Proverbs, they are like "small pictures crowded together on the walls of a large gallery." Read the following verses where the word "proverb(s)" appears:

Numbers 21:27—first appearance of the word in the Bible
1 Samuel 10:12—first citation of a proverb
2 Peter 2:22—a New Testament citation of a biblical proverb

II. AUTHORSHIP

Most of the proverbs originated with Solomon son of David. (Read 1:1, 10:1, and 25:1, which are the opening verses of the three largest sections of the book.) Chapters 30 and 31 are assigned to Agur and Lemuel, respectively, whose identities are unknown.[1] The section 22:17–24:34 is attributed to "the wise men" (22:17; cf. 24:23). Read 1 Kings 4:31 for a reference to such a class of men. If the wise men of Proverbs 22:17 lived before Solomon's time, Solomon may have been the one to assemble their writings and add them to his own. The proverbs of chapters 25-29 were written by Solomon and edited about two hundred years later by a committee appointed by King Hezekiah (c. 700 B.C.). Some think that this group, called 'men of Hezekiah" (25:1), may have included Isaiah and Micah, who were contemporaries of Hezekiah.

Solomon was a unique character in many ways. Consult a Bible dictionary for a sketch of his colorful career. From 1 Kings 3:12 and 4:29 we learn that his wisdom was a direct gift from God. This was in answer to Solomon's petition (1 Kings 3:5-9). Solomon was the author of 3,000 proverbs and 1,005 songs (1 Kings 4:32). Read 1 Kings 3:16-28; 4:29-34; and 10:1-9, noting other things said about him, such as his knowledge of natural science and his wealth.

Solomon is the author of three books of the Bible. One commentator has suggested the possibility of the books' being written at different stages of his career:[2]

1. Song of Solomon—written when he was young, and in love

2. Proverbs—written when he was middle aged, when his intellectual powers were at their peak

3. Ecclesiastes—written in his old age, when he was disappointed and disillusioned with the carnality of much of his life.

III. DATE

As noted above, most of Proverbs was written by Solomon. This would date his work around 950-900 B.C.[3] See Chart A. Hezekiah's collection was formed around 700 B.C. It is reasonable to conclude that the various groups of proverbs were brought together as one book around that date, namely 700 B.C.[4]

1. Some hold that these two names may be poetic references to Solomon himself.
2. John Phillips, *Exploring the Scriptures*, p. 108.
3. The historical background of chapters 1-29, though sparce, corresponds closely to the conditions of Solomon's reign. See G. T. Manley, *The New Bible Handbook*, p. 199. Read Proverbs 29:18; 15:8; 21:3, 27 for references to the law and sacrifices of Israel.
4. This assumes that Agur, Lemuel, and "the wise men," noted earlier, lived no later than Hezekiah.

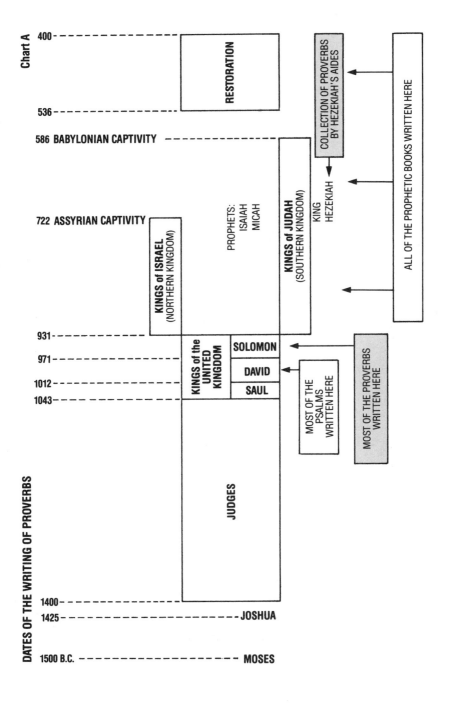

Chart A

DATES OF THE WRITING OF PROVERBS

400 - - - - - - - - - - - - - - -

RESTORATION

536 - - - - - - - - - - - - - - -

586 BABYLONIAN CAPTIVITY - - - - - - - - - - - - - -

COLLECTION OF PROVERBS BY HEZEKIAH'S AIDES

ALL OF THE PROPHETIC BOOKS WRITTEN HERE

KING HEZEKIAH

722 ASSYRIAN CAPTIVITY

KINGS of ISRAEL (NORTHERN KINGDOM)

PROPHETS: ISAIAH MICAH

KINGS of JUDAH (SOUTHERN KINGDOM)

931 - - - - - - - - - - - -

971 - - - - - - - - - - - -

1012 - - - - - - - - - - - -

1043 - - - - - - - - - - - -

KINGS of the UNITED KINGDOM

SOLOMON

DAVID

SAUL

MOST OF THE PSALMS WRITTEN HERE

MOST OF THE PROVERBS WRITTEN HERE

JUDGES

1400 - - - - - - - - - - - -

1425 - - - - - - - - - - - - - - - - - - - JOSHUA

1500 B.C. - - - - - - - - - - - - - - - - - - - MOSES

Refer to Chart A again, and note how close Proverbs and Psalms are as to time of writing. David's psalms give us a vivid view of the worship by God's people before the kingdom's decline, and Solomon's proverbs reflect the zealous concern of believers for a righteous walk. The prophets came later, during the years of Israel's apostasy and idolatry, to call the people to a saving knowledge of God.

IV. PURPOSES

The proverbs are God's detailed instructions and exhortations to His people concerning their thought-and-deed life. Much of the book is addressed especially to young people (e.g., 1:4, 8). The proverbs are mainly about personal ethics, not as the sinner's way to God but as the believer's walk with God on this earth. But though the book is not intended to elaborate on the way of salvation, such key phrases as "the fear of the Lord"(1:7) tell basically how a sinner is brought into fellowship with God. The counsel of Proverbs is profitable for all people, saved and unsaved, but the unsaved cannot claim salvation by doing its good deeds. "For by grace are ye saved through faith; and that not of yourselves: it is the gift of God: not of works, lest any man should boast" (Eph. 2:8-9).

Read 1:2-4, and note the book's own statement of its purpose: to impart wisdom. This wisdom is not mere head knowledge but divinely enlightened understanding of what is good and what is evil (1 Kings 3:9), and an experiential knowledge of the Lord personally.

Solomon also wrote about the purpose of his proverbs in Ecclesiastes 12:9-14. Compare this passage with the phrase "instruction in righteousness" of 2 Timothy 3:16.

One cannot help but by impressed after reading Proverbs that God is so vitally interested in the smallest details of the daily walk of His children. This is our God, our Creator, our Saviour, and our Lord!

V. PLACE IN THE BIBLE

Although isolated proverbs appear in different books of the Bible, Proverbs is unique among the sixty-six books. In the English canon it is the third of the five poetical books. Chart B shows comparisons of its contents with that of other Old Testament books.

Kenneth Taylor has written this testimony about his experience when composing the paraphrases of Psalms, Proverbs, and the Prophets for *The Living Bible*:

books	keynotes	uses
Books of the Law	revelation and guidance	manual of history and legislation
Books of the Prophets	authority	message for today and tomorrow
Job	questions and reasonings	answers from God and men
Psalms	worship	handbook of devotion
Proverbs	observation and reflection	guide to practical living

Then something happened. For these marvelous portions of the Word of God have become my meat and drink! Now I ask sincerely how anyone can live without these precious messages of hope and trust. It's true that other parts of the Bible give the same assurance, warnings, and joy—but no others are quite like the Psalms; no others have such exciting, thoughtful wisdom as the Proverbs. No others contain the awesome pathos of the Prophets.[5]

The New Testament writers quote and allude to Proverbs several times. Read the references listed on the following page.

One book of the New Testament concentrates on the conduct of believers, just as Proverbs does in the Old Testament. That book is the epistle of James. In fact, James is sometimes referred to as the "Proverbs of the New Testament."

Can you recall things Jesus spoke that were similar to these proverbs:

25:6-7

_____

14:11

_____

27:1

_____

The relation of Proverbs to Christ is deeper than appears on the surface. Some see Christ foreshadowed in such explicit passages

5. Kenneth N. Taylor, Preface to _Living Psalms and Proverbs_ (Wheaton, Ill.:Tyndale, 1967).

PROVERBS	N.T. QUOTE OR ALLUSION
3:7	Romans 12:16
25:21-22	Romans 12:20
3:34	James 4:6
24:21	1 Peter 2:17
16:7	1 Peter 3:13
11:31	1 Peter 4:18
26:11	2 Peter 2:22
3:11-12	Hebrews 12:5-6
4:26	Hebrews 12:13
10:12	1 Peter 4:8
22:9	2 Corinthians 9:7
25:6-7	Luke 14:10

as 8:22-31; 23:11; and 30:4. A foundational connection is that the wisdom spoken of in Proverbs is found completely in Christ (1 Cor. 1:30). "The aspiration in Proverbs is for wisdom to become incarnate (Prov. 8), as indeed it did when 'all the treasures of wisdom and knowledge' became flesh in Christ (Col. 2:3)."[6] The "wise" man of Proverbs is the righteous man, and no man is righteous except as he is clothed with the righteousness of Christ. So the truly wise man today is the born-again Christian.

VI. LITERARY CHARACTERISTICS

Any reader of Proverbs quickly observes that its style and content are different from other parts of the Bible, such as Genesis or Matthew. Let us look at the various literary characteristics of this book. This will help us in our later studies.

A. Type

Proverbs is classified as "wisdom literature." (Other wisdom books are Job, Ecclesiastes, and parts of Psalms.) In Old Testament times Israel was ruled by judges and kings and was ministered to

6. Norman L. Geisler, *Christ: The Theme of the Bible* (Chicago: Moody, 1968), p. 96.

by such groups as priests, prophets, scribes, historians, singers, and "wise men," or philosophers. King David was both a king and singer. His son Solomon was both a king and philosopher. Hebrew "wise men" were usually elders associated with schools of wisdom, who shared their practical views of life and the world with their Jewish brethren. The following comparisons of the three groups, prophets, priests, and wise men (see Jer. 18:18), show how practical the wise men were:[7]

HEBREW PROPHET, PRIEST, AND PHILOSOPHER COMPARED

Subject	PROPHET	PRIEST	PHILOSOPHER
righteousness	It is just	It is commanded	It is prudent
sin	It is disobedience	It is defilement	It is folly

B. Style

The following descriptions show the variety of styles and forms in which the proverbs appear:
1. *Various forms.* The forms are: poetry, brief parables, sharp questions, minute stories. For two examples of poems, read the following:
   1:20-33 "Wisdom's Cry of Warning" (a dramatic monologue)
   3:1-10 "The Commandment and Reward" (a sonnet)
2. *Common devices.* The devices are:
   antithesis: comparing opposite things (16:22)
   comparison: comparing similar things (17:10)
   imagery: using picture language (26:27)
   personification: assigning personality to an inanimate thing (9:1)
3. *Prominent teaching method.* The prominent method is contrast. Scan chapters 10-15, and note the repeated word "but." Gleason Archer writes,

> The constant preoccupation of the book is with the elemental antagonisms of obedience versus rebellion, industry versus laziness, prudence versus presumption, and so on. These are so

7. See W. Graham Scroggie, *Know Your Bible*, 1:128.

presented as to put before the reader a clear-cut choice, leaving him no ground for wretched compromise or vacillating indecision.[8]

4. *Length.* Unit proverbs are one to four verses, and clusters are groups of unit proverbs. In the early chapters the common unit proverb is one verse. An example of a cluster is the passage about fools in 26:1-12.

5. *Symmetry.* Most of the proverbs are symmetrical (e.g., the antithetical maxims of two lines connected by the word "but"). But Hebrew writers were not bound by symmetry. "Modern hands itch to smooth away irregularities—often overlooking the fact that an asymmetrical proverb can be richer than a symmetrical."[9]

Proverb-type writings were not exclusively Israel's. Archaeologists have uncovered proverbs of other nations as well.[10] The main difference is not in style but in content. Compare the following two proverbs. What is the notable difference?

a. "Do not lean on the scales, nor falsify the weights, nor damage the fractions of the measure" (proverb of Amen-em-ope of Egypt).

b. "Divers weights, and divers measures, both of them are alike abomination to the Lord" (proverb of Solomon, 20:10).

VII. SUGGESTIONS FOR INTERPRETATION

Before we can apply a passage of Scripture, we first need to interpret the passage, that is, learn what it means. This follows the order: observation first, then interpretation, then application. Here are some suggestions for interpreting the maxims of Proverbs:

1. Recognize that the proverbs are instructions from the Lord, not mere secular maxims. It is not by accident that the name *Lord* (Jehovah) appears eighty-six times in the book.

2. Interpret "wisdom" in the book as righteousness or holiness, which describes the heart of that person who truly knows God. Likewise interpret such words as "fool" and "folly" as meaning wickedness of the unsaved man.

3. Recognize the device of personification whenever it appears in the book. For example, the foolish woman of 9:13-15 is

---

8. Gleason L. Archer, *A Survey of Old Testament Introduction*, p. 452.
9. Derek Kidner, *The Proverbs*, p. 28.
10. There is strong evidence that pagan writers even borrowed from the canonical Proverbs for their own purposes. See W. Jones and Andrew Walls, "The Proverbs," in *The New Bible Commentary*, ed. F. Davidson, p. 516.

not primarily an individual person as such, but spiritual folly or wickedness (the opposite of spiritual wisdom, or righteousness).

4. Let the surrounding verses shed light on a proverb when its meaning is unclear. However, because of the miscellaneous character of the listings of many proverbs, it may be necessary to refer to more distant verses (e.g., in another chapter or even in another book) where a similar phrase appears, for its clarification. (For example, the phrase "strange woman" in 20:16 is partly explained by 2:16.) An exhaustive concordance is a valuable help here.

5. When the most obvious interpretation of a proverb seems to contradict another Scripture, seek its deeper meaning. (Cf. Prov. 10:27 and Gen. 4:8; and Prov. 16:7 and Acts 14:19.)

6. If a proverb is unclear or ambiguous in the King James Version, compare the reading of a modern paraphrase.[11]

7. Let the key verse 1:7 be the controller of all your interpretations of the many proverbs of this book of God.

VIII. APPLYING PROVERBS

Proverbs is filled with commands and exhortations about daily conduct. The reader has hardly begun when he is confronted with such words as "If sinners entice thee, consent thou not" (1:10). God knew that His people would need to be reminded again and again about how to think, speak, and act, so He inspired the writing and collection of Proverbs. No Christian today can afford to neglect its counsel.

As noted earlier, Proverbs does *not* teach salvation by works. It *does* teach the righteous works of a saved person. It does not include much doctrine. It does emphasize practice. One writer describes its Christian purpose thus:

> While other parts of Scripture show us the glory of our high calling, this may instruct in all minuteness of detail how to 'walk worthy of it.' Elsewhere we learn our completeness in Christ (Col ii.10); and most justly we glory in our high exaltation as "joint heirs with Christ," etc.
>
> (Rom. viii.17; Eph. ii.6). We look into this book, and, as by the aid of the microscope, we see the minuteness of our Christian obligations; that there is not a temper, a look, a word, a move-

11. Modern paraphrases are the interpretations of those writing the paraphrases. They are not intended to by a word-for-word translation of the Bible text. One of the main purposes of a paraphrase is to clarify an ambiguous word or phrase of the Bible text.

ment, the most important action of the day, the smallest relative duty, in which we do not either deface or adorn the image of our Lord, and the profession of His name.[12]

Proverbs truly shows how the believer "may adorn the doctrine of God our Saviour in all things" (Titus 2:10). A Christian who applies Proverbs consistently is more than a Sunday-go-to-church Christian. His faith will show forth at the office or shop, in a traffic jam, at the store counter, when meeting a stranger on the street, at the supper table or voting booth, and before a television set.

More than a hundred yours ago this was the testimony of a Scotsman:

> The day was in Scotland when all her children were initiated into the art of reading through the Book of Proverbs. . . . I have no doubt whatever . . . that the high character which Scotsmen earned in bygone years was mainly due to their early acquaintance with the Proverbs.[13]

Even unbelievers recognize the value of Proverbs as a manual for conduct. How much more should it apply to Christians, who have the indwelling Spirit to help them live the life it describes?

Some of the best illustrations of the truth of the biblical proverbs are to be found in the lives of Bible characters. Listed below are names that might be associated with the proverb cited. Do you recall any experiences of each person, illustrating the proverb?

10:7*a*—Elisha, Dorcas
10:7*b*—Cain, Balaam, Jezebel, Judas Iscariot
16:18—Nebuchadnezzar, Herod Agrippa

Observe that Proverbs contains thirty-one chapters, which is the number of days of many of our months. Why not try reading one chapter a day, as a daily spiritual tonic? This is the testimony of Billy Graham:

> For a number of years, I have made it a practice to read five Psalms and one chapter of Proverbs a day. The Psalms teach us how to get along with God, and the Proverbs teach us how to get along with our fellowmen. . . . Reading this much in each book regularly takes me through them once each month. You

12. Otto Zockler, *Commentary of The Holy Scriptures, Proverbs*, ed. John Peter Lange, p. 3.
13. Quoted in ibid., p. 4.

cannot imagine the blessing this encounter with the Scriptures has been in my life, especially in recent years.[14]

Refer to the Appendix for a list of familiar proverbs.

IX. A CONCLUDING THOUGHT

H. A. Ironside once wrote that the soul that most deeply enters into the reality of the new creation in Christ will most appreciate the instruction of this great practical book of the Bible, Proverbs.[15] As you prepare your heart to study this book of God, why not thank Him again for His interest in the smallest details of your daily life, and claim the power of the Holy Spirit to obey His instruction?

14. Billy Graham, Introduction to *Living Psalms and Proverbs*.
15. H. A. Ironside, *Notes on the Book of Proverbs*, p. 10.

Lesson 2
Survey of the Book of Proverbs

Survey study of a book of the Bible should always precede detailed analysis of its parts. There are more than 900 verses in Proverbs, most of which are similar in form. So it is easy to see how one studying the book could lose momentum rather quickly if he has not already gained an overall perspective of the book. The purpose of this lesson is to get a skyscraper view of Proverbs, scanning its highlights and general structure without tarrying over many details.

I. OVERALL THEME

Recall the overall theme of Proverbs from Lesson 1. You have read a fair number of miscellaneous proverbs so that you have a "feel" for the book. In your own words, what is Proverbs trying to say?

II. MAIN DIVISIONS

Read the first verse of each chapter of the book. At what points do headings or titles appear? Compare your observations with the list given below. Record the heading opposite each reference.
1:1

_____

10:1

_____

25:1

_____

In addition to the above divisional points, one is suggested by
22:17. Read the verse.
Most books of the Bible have an introduction and a conclusion. What about Proverbs? Begin reading chapter 1. How many
verses would you identify as an introduction?
The identification of a conclusion is more difficult. The last
segment is about a virtuous woman (31:10-31). If this is not the
conclusion, then the previous segment should be included (31:1-
9). But if 31:1 is part of the conclusion, then the similar heading of
30:1 should also be included. Since two full chapters are longer
than a typical conclusion to a book, we may say simply that Proverbs concludes with an epilogue of two supplements (chaps. 30-
31). The introduction then could be called a prologue. Using 1:1-6
as the extent of that introduction, the basic structure of the book
would be this:

1:1	1:7	30:1　　　31:31
PROLOGUE	MAXIMS	EPILOGUE

III. CONTENT OF EACH DIVISION

Chart C shows the various divisions of Proverbs that we have observed thus far and includes outlines of content. Answer the following questions of the basis of the chart:
　　1. Where is the purpose of Proverbs stated?
　　2. What group of chapters develops the primary theme of the
book?
　　3. Where is there a concentration of one-verse proverbs?
　　4. What part of the book is addressed especially to young
people? Confirm your answer by these verses: (1:8; 2:1; 3:1; 4:1;
5:1; 6:1; etc.).
　　5. What groups of chapters are specifically assigned to
Solomon?

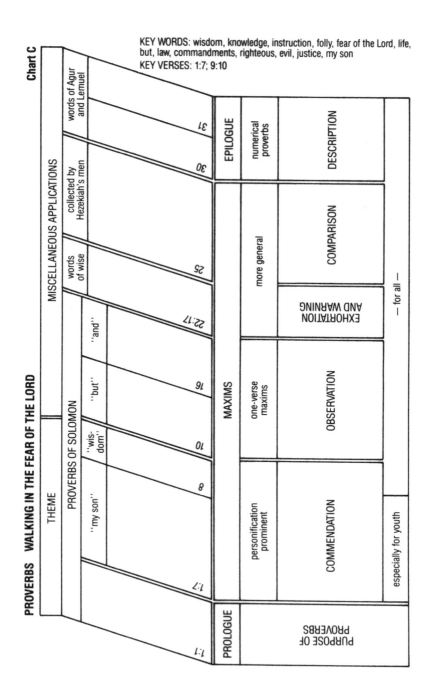

PROVERBS   WALKING IN THE FEAR OF THE LORD

Chart C

KEY WORDS: wisdom, knowledge, instruction, folly, fear of the Lord, life, but, law, commandments, righteous, evil, justice, my son
KEY VERSES: 1:7; 9:10

THEME

PROVERBS OF SOLOMON   MISCELLANEOUS APPLICATIONS

"my son"   "wis-dom"   "but"   "and"   words of wise   collected by Hezekiah's men   words of Agur and Lemuel

1:7   8   10   16   22:17   25   30   31

PROLOGUE   MAXIMS   EPILOGUE

1:1

PURPOSE OF PROVERBS

personification prominent   one-verse maxims   more general   numerical proverbs

COMMENDATION   OBSERVATION   EXHORTATION AND WARNING   COMPARISON   DESCRIPTION

especially for youth   — for all —

20

IV. A KEY VERSE

Chart C shows 1:7 as a key verse, reflected in the title given the book. In the course of your studies be on the lookout for other key verses.

Note also the list of key words. You will probably want to add to this list at later times.

V. VARIETY OF SUBJECTS

The list of different subjects written about in Proverbs seems endless. Here are some examples:[1]

Topics: wisdom, sin, tongue, wealth, pride, idleness, love, pleasure, success, temperance, morals

Contrasting subjects: God and man, time and eternity, truth and falsehood, wealth and poverty, purity and impurity, justice and injustice, pleasure and misery

Evil people: prating fool, talebearer, whisperer, backbiter, false boaster, speculator

Social relations: master and servant, rich and poor, husband and wife, parents and children

Youth: Henrietta C. Mears has compiled this interesting list of proverbs for young people, taken from chapters 1-9, one per chapter.[2] Read the verses:

SERMONS FOR SONS

"Wise Up!" 1:7   "God's Black List" 6:17-19
"Walk Straight!" 2:20   "A Bad Woman" 7:15-27
"Directions" 3:6   "Riches" 8:11
"Watch Your Step!" 4:26   "More Fun!" 9:17-18
"Flee Flattery" 5:3

VI. WORDS TO PONDER

Every word of God is tested;
He is a shield to those who take refuge in Him.
Do not add to His words
Lest He reprove you, and you be proved a liar.
Proverbs 30:5-6, NASB.

---

1. See W. Graham Scroggie, *Know Your Bible*, 1:140-41.
2. Henrietta C. Mears, *What the Bible Is All About*, p. 196.

Lesson 3

The Beginning of Wisdom

With this lesson we begin our analysis of the text of Proverbs'
thirty-one chapters. In chapter 1 the first six verses are the
book's introduction, or prologue. Then follows a key verse of the
book, verse 7, and the first of several messages addressed to "my
son."

The first chapter of any book informs the reader what to expect in the remainder of the work. Thus it is important to spend a
little extra time in this opening chapter of Proverbs to catch its
purpose, feel its tone, and enter into its momentum. We would do
well to apply Solomon's counsel even to the study of the book: "A
wise man will hear" (1:5).

I. PREPARATION FOR STUDY

Since the subject of wisdom is prominent in Proverbs, it would be
helpful before studying chapter 1 to see how the word *wisdom*
and related words are used by New Testament writers. Read the
passages cited below:
1. *Colossians 1:9-10*: What is meant by each of these words in
verse 9:
Knowledge

_____

Wisdom

_____

Understanding

_____

Verse 10 is about the believer's *walk*. How is this related to the
subject of wisdom in verse 9?

PROLOGUE	1	
KEY VERSE	7	
FIRST MESSAGE	8	
	20	repentance
	23	rejection
	26	recompense
	28	rejection
	33	

2. *James 3:13-18*: What two kinds of wisdom are described here? How does verse 17 describe one of these?

In view of your study of these New Testament passages, how would you define and describe wisdom?

II. ANALYSIS

Segment to be analyzed: 1:1-33
Stanza divisions: at verses 1, 7, 8, 20

A. General Analysis

There are three main parts to this segment, as shown on the work sheet of Chart D (see narrow left-hand column). Scan the chapter with these parts in mind, after you have marked the stanza divisions (shown above) in your Bible. How does verse 1 serve as a title for the book? How does verse 7 serve as a theme verse? How do the words "My son" (1:8) identify the readers addressed?

Use Chart D to record various observations and outlines that you make in the course of your study.

B. Stanza Analysis

1. *Prologue: 1:1-6.* The first four verses of this prologue are an extended heading, not a grammatical sentence. Note the repeated word "to." The following paraphrases of the *Amplified Bible* show a clearer rendering of this preposition:

v. 1: "The Proverbs of Solomon the son of David, king of Israel"

vv. 2-3: "that people may know"

v. 4: "that prudence may be given to the simple"

The preposition "to" at the beginning of verse 6 connects the verse closely to the previous one. Here is how *The Living Bible*

verb	object
know	wisdom instruction

24

paraphrases the two verses: "I want those already wise to become the wiser and become leaders by exploring the depths of meaning in these nuggets of truth."

One obvious feature of this stanza is the frequent appearance of words like "wisdom" and "understanding." Make a list of these, together with the verbs with which they are linked (examples are given):

Note: The phrase "justice . . . judgment . . . equity" (v. 3) is accurately translated "righteousness, justice, and integrity" (*Amplified Bible*). Compare 2:9. Also, subtlety is better translated "insight." What does each word mean to you? For help in interpretation, read paraphrases of modern versions. How often does the word "wisdom" (or "wise") appear in the stanza? It is important at the beginning of your study of Proverbs to know the full meaning of this word, for it appears throughout the book. Recall what was said about "wisdom" in Lesson 1. (See II. Notes concerning other words of the above list.)

2. *Key verse: 1:7.* This is the opening proverb of the book. It tells the theme of the book. (The purpose of Proverbs was given in the prologue). What are the two opposite ways, or walks, described here? A person reading 1:2-6 may say, "Yes, I would like to have that kind of wisdom. But how can I get it?" What is the answer of 1:7? What do you think is meant by "the fear of the Lord"? Compare 2:5; 9:10; 14:27; 23:17.

3. *The phrase "my son": 1:8-19.* In what verse does the phrase "my son" appear? What is the main point of each of these three parts:

1:8-9

_____

_____

1:10-14

_____

_____

1:15-19

_____

_____

What phrase of 1:19 describes the sin of 1:10-18?

4. *Call to repentance: 1:20-33.* Mark divisions in your Bible as they appear on Chart D. Read the passage section by section, following this outline:

call to repentance	1:20-22
man's rejection of God	1:23-25

25

recompense   1:26-27
God's rejection of man   1:28-32
invitation repeated   1:33

According to verse 20, who is the speaker of these verses? Whom does "she" personify? In view of the content of 1:20-33, what does the word "wisdom" signify? Compare 1 Corinthians 1:24. Also read Isaiah 11:1-5, and note similar attributes ascribed to the Messiah.

Analyze in more detail the five parts of this stanza as shown in the above outline. Record observations on the work sheet of Chart D. Among other things look for answers to these questions:

(a) What three kinds of unbelievers are referred to in 1:22?

(b) Compare the three phrases of 1:23 beginning with the word "my." What do you see of God's grace here?

(c) Is God made happy when He must bring judgment upon people? How do you explain the words "laugh" and "mock" in verse 26?

(d) Can God's gracious invitation be spurned to the point where it is permanently withdrawn? Does 1:28-32 support your answer?

(e) What are the invitation and promise of 1:33?

III. NOTES

1. *"Instruction"* (1:2). This is teaching by discipline. The root of the Hebrew word is "chastise." Compare 13:24, where the same Hebrew word appears.

2. *"Simple"* (1:4). The Hebrew word comes from a root meaning "to leave oneself open." Such a "simple" man is one who flirts with sin and yields quickly to satanic enticement. The word "entice" of 1:10 is from the same root as "simple."

3. *"Wise counsels"* (1:5). The Hebrew root suggests the idea of a steersman. Hence these translations:

    "attain to leadership" (Berkeley)
    "become leaders" (TLB[1])

4. *"Fools"* (1:7). Of all the books of the Bible, this word appears most often in Proverbs (see an exhaustive concordance). Consistently it represents the sinner. (Read 14:9.) The Greek translation of the Old Testament (Septuagint) translates the word as "ungodly."

5. *"Instruction of thy father ... law of the mother"* (1:8). This is not primarily a reference to parental advice as such, but to god-

1. *The Living Bible.*

26

ly parents' instruction and application of God's Word in the raising of their children.

IV. FOR THOUGHT AND DISCUSSION

1. In Proverbs the word "hear" usually connotes the stronger response of obedience. (For example, the Hebrew word translated "hear" in Proverbs 1:5 is translated "obey" in Deuteronomy 11:27.) What part does obedience play in a person's salvation and in his Christian walk?

2. What help can Christian parents receive from the Bible for raising their children in the fear of the Lord?

3. "Consent thou not" (1:10). What power does the Christian have to resist sinful enticements of the world?

4. Some people do not believe in eternal hell because their concept of a loving God contradicts this. How would you answer such an objection?

5. What attitude of fear should a Christian have in his daily walk? What fears need he not carry?

6. How can you as a believer grow in the wisdom that Solomon writes about?

V. FURTHER STUDY

1. Study the phrase "fear of the Lord" as it appears throughout Proverbs and other books of the Bible (e.g., Psalms.) Consult an exhaustive concordance for help in this.

2. You may want to spend more time studying the word "wisdom" and the similar words of 1:1-6 as these occur in the Bible.

VI. WORDS TO PONDER

Only fools refuse to be taught (1:7*b*, TLB).

Lesson 4

Proverbs 2:1–4:27

"Wisdom Is the Principal Thing"

Again and again Solomon exhorts his son, the reader, to hear and heed the instruction of Wisdom. This appeal is repeated for nine full chapters before the long list of miscellaneous proverbs begins in chapter 10. Why the repetition? The answer is not hard to find. Solomon wisely knows that commands and exhortations about daily conduct are meaningless to one whose heart attitude is not right before God. Hence his constant appeal in the early chapters for an attitude of submission and teachableness, suggested by such words as "hear, receive, seek, forget not, attend to." This relation between chapters 1-9 and the remainder of the book

CONTEXT OF CHAPTERS 1-9 **Chart E**

CHAPS. 1-9		CHAPS. 10-31
COUNSEL ABOUT WISDOM		PROVERBS ABOUT DAILY LIVING
FEAR	**HEAR**	**DO**
THE LORD	INSTRUCTION	➡ DEEDS OF RIGHTEOUSNESS
Attitude of Worship	Attitude of Obedience	

is shown on Chart E. Keep this in mind as you study the remainder of Proverbs, to give perspective to your detailed analyses.[1]

I. PREPARATION FOR STUDY

1. Read Colossians 2:6. What is the connection between the words "received" and "walk"? Compare this with the outline shown on Chart E.

2. What are your thoughts about the responsibility and accountability of the following:

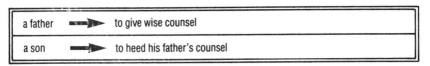

| a father | ➡ | to give wise counsel |
| a son | ➡ | to heed his father's counsel |

Do you think it is important *how* a father gives his son advice? As you study the passage of this lesson try to observe emotion or feeling in Solomon's counsel.

3. Always keep in mind what the word "wisdom" means in Proverbs.

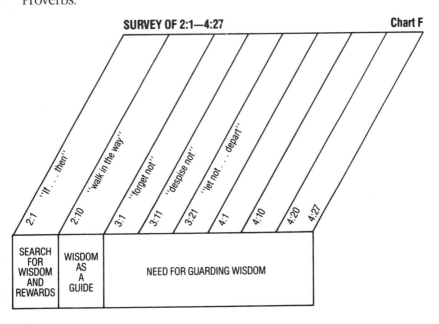

SURVEY OF 2:1—4:27   Chart F

"if . . . then"   "walk in the way"   ". . forget not"   ". . despise not"   ". . let not . . . depart"

2:1   2:10   3:1   3:11   3:21   4:1   4:10   4:20   4:27

| SEARCH FOR WISDOM AND REWARDS | WISDOM AS A GUIDE | NEED FOR GUARDING WISDOM |

1. As noted in Lesson 3, the word "hear" in Proverbs has the connotation of obedience. This is shown on Chart E. Compare Jesus' use of the word in Matthew 13:13.

II. ANALYSIS

Passage to by analyzed: 2:1–4:27
Stanza divisions: at verses 2:1, 10; 3:1, 11, 21; 4:1, 10, 20

A. General Analysis

Chart F breaks down this segment into its eight stanzas, showing an outline on the subject as *"wisdom."*[2] Also shown on the chart are key phrases of the Bible text. Add other key phrases in the three blank spaces. Keep this chart before you as you read the segment the first time.

B. Stanza Analysis

1. *Stanza 2:1-9.* Analyze these verses around the following structure (record phrases of the text):

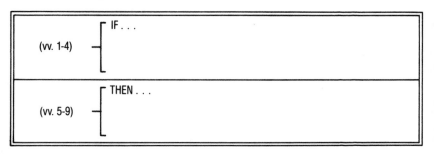

How many times does the word "if" appear in verses 1-4? How often does the word "then" appear in verses 5-9?
Compare the various verbs of verses 1-4.

Compare the phrases that follow the word "then."

---

2. Actually, it is difficult to detect a logical progression of thought in the segment. This is typical of most of the book, as we observed in our earlier survey.

30

Compare 2:9 and 1:3

_____

_____

Did you notice other similarities between this stanza and 1:2-6?

_____

Note the two names of God in 2:5. The name "Lord" translates the Hebrew *Jehovah* and appears eighty-six times in the book. It is the name that identified God as the Saviour of Israel, the Covenant-maker, and the Covenant-fulfiller. The name "God" translates *Elohim*, a name of majesty and authority. It is the first reference to God in the Bible (Gen. 1:1). In Proverbs the name "God" appears only eight times. Can you think of a reason that Solomon would use the name *Jehovah* much more often than *Elohim?*

_____

Compare the two phrases "fear of the Lord" and "knowledge of God" (2:5).

_____

Why not this arrangement: "fear of God" and "knowledge of the Lord"?

_____

2. *Stanza 2:10-22.* In these lines wisdom is shown as a guide. Compare the two *ways* of verses 12 and 20:
    "to deliver thee from the way of the evil man"
    "that thou mayest walk in the way of good men"
How does the stanza describe each of these ways?

_____

_____

How is wisdom shown to be the believer's guide?

_____

What verses are about "the strange woman"?

_____

Whom does she represent in everyday life?

_____

Summarize the contents of chapter 2 using this outline:

THE WAY OF GOOD MEN (v. 20)

    A. Desire   (2:1-9)
    B. Deliverance   (2:10-19)
    C. Dwelling   (2:20-22)

3. *Stanzas 3:1–4:27.* Recall from Chart F that this section is about "The Need for Guarding Wisdom." As you study each stanza you may want to record key proverbs, that is, those that strike you as being especially significant (e.g., 3:5-6). Locate the following words and phrases in the text, and observe what the context says about each. Record your findings.

"my law"

_____

"favor . . . in the sight of God and man"

_____

"thy substance"

_____

"correction"

_____

"pleasantness"

_____

"life unto thy soul"

_____

"sleep shall be sweet"

_____

"he giveth grace"

_____

The three stanzas of chapter 4 may be analyzed together around the common subject of wisdom. Chart G is a partly completed analytical chart showing a few parts of this chapter. Use the chart as a work sheet to record your own observations as you study. For example, record the many promises of the chapter; also references to "keep."

How does Solomon's autobiographical testimony (4:3ff.) strengthen his counsel to others?

_____

The quote of his father David's words begins at verse 4.
Where do you think the quote ends?

_____

What parts of the body are referred to in 4:20-27?

_____

_____

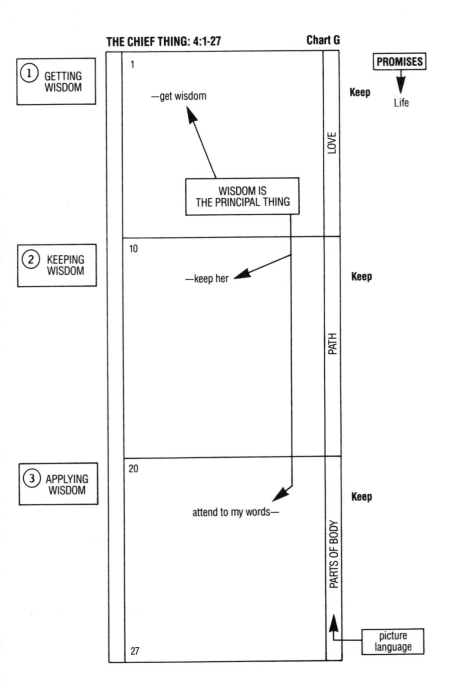

What is the main point?

III. NOTES

1. *"Strange woman . . . stranger"* (2:16). These are references to an immoral woman. (See 5:20.) Various versions translate the words as "prostitute," "adulteress," "loose woman."
2. *"Forget not my law"* (3:1). In the original setting Solomon here was urging his son to obey his instructions. A son's obedience to his father is thus being taught. (Cf. Eph. 6:2.) But the essence of Solomon's instruction was God's Word. Read Deuteronomy 6:6-7, which Solomon certainly obeyed. So such references in Proverbs as "my law" or "my commandments" can rightly be interpreted in their deepest significance as God's law and God's commandments.
3. *"New wine"* (3:10). R. Laird Harris writes of this:

> The Hebrew has two words for wine. *Yayin*, which means fermented wine, is used in the condemnatory passage in Prov 23:31-35. *Tirosh*, used here as the fresh product of the pressing, is properly . . . grape juice.[3]

4. *"The principal thing"* (4:7). The word translated "principal" means *the first*, in time, rank, or place. Some translators take it as a time reference: "The beginning of wisdom."[4] The King James and *American Standard* versions translate the word as describing rank, thus "principal," or "primary." This seems to be the more natural reading in this context. Compare the same use in Exodus 30:23.

IV. FOR THOUGHT AND DISCUSSION

1. What does 3:9 teach about the believer's stewardship? What is the meaning of "firstfruits of all thine increase"? Read Deuteronomy 26 in this connection. What is the relation of tithing to the Christian life?
2. What is God's purpose in chastening His children, according to 3:11-12? Have you experienced His chastening?

3. R. Laird Harris, "Proverbs," in *The Wycliffe Bible Commentary*, ed. Charles F. Pfeiffer and Everett Harrison, p. 560.
4. For example, see the Berkeley version and the NASB.

3. Think more about the parts of the body mentioned in 4:20-27. Derive some practical lessons from this passage, in connection with each member.

V. FURTHER STUDY

With the help of an exhaustive concordance read the various references to "woman" in chapter 1-9. Why are all the references in this section about *evil* women?

VI. WORDS TO PONDER

In everything you do, put God first, and he will direct you and crown your efforts with success (3:6, TLB).

Lesson 5

Enticement to Sin

The lure of sexual impurity has been a besetting problem of young people throughout the ages. So it does not surprise us that Solomon wrote much about evil adulteresses enticing his young son to give away his honor. Needless to say, Solomon's counsel is just as appropriate today as it was 3,000 years ago.

Most of the passage of this lesson is about the particular sin of adultery (e.g., 6:26). The passage can be applied, however, to all kinds of sin, because Satan uses subtle enticement in all of his temptings.

I. PREPARATION FOR STUDY

Solomon's parents, David and Bathsheba, had committed the sin of adultery that Solomon warned about in Proverbs. Read 2 Samuel 11-12 for the tragic story of this time in David's life. The two sins of adultery and murder marked a turning point in David's career.

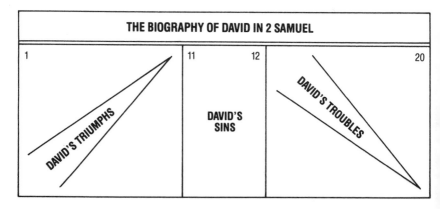

THE BIOGRAPHY OF DAVID IN 2 SAMUEL

1   11   12   20

DAVID'S TRIUMPHS

DAVID'S SINS

DAVID'S TROUBLES

He was never the same again. As long as he lived, troubles kept arising to plague him. This is shown in the survey of 2 Samuel on the previous page.

Do you think Solomon may have pondered the sins of his parents as he wrote about the subject to his own son?

II. ANALYSIS

Passage to be analyzed: 5:1–7.27
Stanza divisions: at verses 5:1, 15; 6:1, 6, 12, 20; 7:1, 6, 24

A. General Analysis

Chart H shows the general structure of this passage. Study the chart carefully, and then scan the Bible text with this pattern in mind.

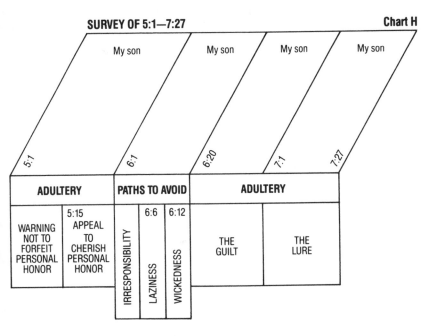

SURVEY OF 5:1—7:27   **Chart H**

ADULTERY		PATHS TO AVOID			ADULTERY	
WARNING NOT TO FORFEIT PERSONAL HONOR	5:15 APPEAL TO CHERISH PERSONAL HONOR	IRRESPONSIBILITY	6:6 LAZINESS	6:12 WICKEDNESS	THE GUILT	THE LURE

Observe the following:

1. The phrase "My son" appears at the beginning of each of four main sections.[1]

---

1. The phrase "O ye children," which may be translated, "O sons," appears at 5:7 and 7:24.

2. Most of the passage is about the adulterous woman ("strange woman").

The section 6:1-19, about other sins, falls between the two "adultery" sections. Can you account for such a detour or interruption? Could 5:22-23 be considered an introduction to 6:1-19?

B. Stanza Analysis

1. *Stanza 5:1-14.* Note how this and the following stanza are represented on Chart H. Observe (1) command, (2) purpose, and (3) reason in verses 1-3.

Which of the three subjects is expanded in the rest of the stanza?

What are the three places in the stanza where reference is made to instruction?

What is meant by the phrase "give thine honour unto others" (5:9)?

2. *Stanza 5:15-23.* The key phrase of this stanza is "thine own." Note its appearances, as well as the repeated word "thy." What is Solomon appealing to here?

What verse indicates that Solomon's "son" was a married man?

What is the sobering truth of 5:21?

3. *Stanza 6:1-19.* What is the subject of each of the three paragraphs?

Study carefully the list of seven "abominations" of 6:16-19. What is meant by "abomination"?

What is intended by the phrase "These six . . . yea, seven" (6:16)?

Note that the seventh sin listed, that of sowing discord, is the sin described just before the list begins (see 6:14-15. Do you see any suggestion of an adulterous heart in the descriptions of this stanza? Is so, there is a continuity of thought between this stanza and the section that follows.

4. *Stanza 6:20-35.* What different things are written here about the guilt and penalties of adultery?

What will help guard a man in the hour of temptation, according to this stanza?

5. *Stanza 7:1-27.* Compare the first five verses of this stanza with the opening verses of 6:20-24. Compare the prostitute's heart and ways with the description of 6:12-14. One writer has described the harlot as "shuffling, dusk-loving, seductive." What is Solomon's purpose in describing in detail a harlot's enticement of a young man?

Compare 7:27 and James 1:14-15.

Write a list of practical lessons that can be learned from this important passage.

III. NOTES

1. *"Thy flesh and thy body are consumed"* (5:11). *The Living Bible* paraphrases this as "syphilis consumes your body."
2. *"Let thy fountains be dispersed"* (5:16). Most versions translate this as a question: "Should thy fountains .. ?" The meaning is, "Why should you beget children with women of the street?" (TLB).
3. *"Six things . . . yea, seven"* (6:16). This literary device of listing things may be intended to put emphasis on the seventh, or last, ti.ing mentioned. (Cf. 6:19 and 6: 14-15.)

4. *"This day have I paid my vows"* (7:14). The woman had fulfilled her formal religious duties and so felt free to indulge in any sinful pleasure.

5. *"I have peace offerings with me"* (7:14). If the prostitute meant these words literally, she was telling the young man that she had plenty of food at her house, left over from the peace offering made at the Temple (cf. Lev. 7:11ff.). *The Living Bible* suggests a figurative meaning with this paraphrase: "I've decided to forget our quarrel."

6. *"Straightway"* (7:22). The word is correctly translated "suddenly."

IV. FOR THOUGHT AND DISCUSSION

1. What have you learned from this passage of Proverbs to help you counsel and advise young people about Satan's sexual allurements?

2. Why is it important to keep God's Word in the heart as a living and powerful force? (See 7:1-3.)

3. Jesus said, "Whosoever looketh on a woman to lust after her hath committed adultery with her already in his heart" (Matt. 5:28). Compare these words with Proverbs 6:25. What is your definition of sin?

4. Read 1 Corinthians 10:12. Is a believer immune from committing such sins as adultery? Read the tragic downfall of Solomon, brought about by his ways with "strange women" (1 Kings 11:1-13). What do you learn from this?

5. If you are studying in a group, discuss the seven sins of 6:16-19.

V. FURTHER STUDY

1. The Hebrew word *atsel* appears sixteen times in Proverbs. Sometimes it is translated "sluggard," sometimes "the slothful one." With the help of a concordance make a word study of this subject.

2. Refer to various commentaries for background to the passage about surety (6:1-5). Also read Paul's epistle to Philemon, observing how Paul was surety for Onesimus (e.g., Philem. 17-18).

VI. WORDS TO PONDER

God is closely watching you, and he weighs carefully everything you do (5:21, TLB).

Lesson 6

Proverbs 8:1–9:18

Call to Righteousness

The closing picture of chapter 7 was dark, painted by such words as "wounded," "hell," and "death." That is precisely where the gospel applies. For "where sin abounded, grace did much more abound: that as sin hath reigned unto death, even so might grace reign through righteousness unto eternal life by Jesus Christ our Lord" (Rom. 5:20-21). The lure of the woman of sin in chapters 5-7 is now contrasted in chapters 8-9 by the bright invitation of the woman of righteousness. Her name is Wisdom, and those who follow her reap untold blessings. These two chapters are a glowing conclusion to the first main division of Proverbs.

I. PREPARATION FOR STUDY

1. Chart I shows the main divisions of Proverbs. This is an excerpt of the main survey Chart C. Note where the two chapters of this lesson appear on the outline.

CONTEXT OF CHAPTERS 8-9 Chart I

1:1	1:7	10:1	22:17	25:1	30:1
PROLOGUE					EPILOGUE
INTRODUCTION	COMMENDATION —praise of wisdom—	OBSERVATION	EXHORTATION AND WARNING	COMPARISON	DESCRIPTION
THE WAY OF WISDOM (RIGHTEOUSNESS)					

41

2. To appreciate fully the message of chapters 8-9, recall what you studied in the last lesson about the harlot. Compare her with the woman called Wisdom (8:1–9:18), and record your notes on the following work sheet:

THE TWO WOMEN OF 5:1—9:18 COMPARED			
	The woman of chapters 5-7		The woman of chapters 8-9
IDENTIFICATION	6:26		8:1, 12
	7:5		
LOCATION	7:12		8:2-3
MESSAGE	7:5		8:6-8
PROMISES	7:18		8:21
			8:35
			9:11
OUTCOME:	7:26-27		8:35
LIFE OR DEATH			9:6, 11

3. Recall from your earlier studies in Proverbs how the words "wise" and "wisdom" are used in this book. (Read 1:20-23.) This wisdom is of the spiritual realm and involves "discernment" between good and evil, and the "commitment" to good, or godliness (1:29)., Whenever you study the word "wisdom" in Proverbs, think "righteousness," and you will be on the right track. Likewise interpret the opposite word "foolish" (and similar words) as "evil."

4. It is interesting to note that the word "wisdom" appears early in the epistle of James, which is sometimes called the "Proverbs of the New Testament." Read James 1:5.

II. ANALYSIS

Passage to be analyzed: 8:1–9:18
Stanza divisions: at verses 8:1, 12, 22, 32; 9:1, 13

A. General Analysis

Chart J shows the six stanzas of this passage. Note the relationships between these stanzas: the first and fourth; second and third; fifth and sixth.

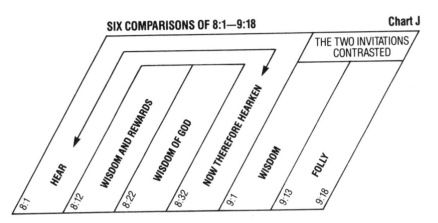

SIX COMPARISONS OF 8:1—9:18   Chart J

THE TWO INVITATIONS CONTRASTED

HEAR / WISDOM AND REWARDS / WISDOM OF GOD / NOW THEREFORE HEARKEN / WISDOM / FOLLY

8:1 8:12 8:22 8:32 9:1 9:13 9:18

Scan the passage and make other general observations of the structure.

B. Stanza Analysis

1. *Stanza 8:1-11.* In what sense is "hear" a key word of the stanza?

_____

_____

What is emphasized more here: description of wisdom or the details of wisdom's message?

_____

_____

2. *Stanza 8:12-21.* What are the rewards of following wisdom (righteousness)?

_____

_____

_____

Some Bible students see Wisdom in this chapter as a picture of Christ. Read Colossians 2:3 and 1 Corinthians 1:30. Then read the stanza as though Christ is speaking the words.

43

3. *Stanza 8:22-31.* How is wisdom related to God in these verses?

What is the main theme of this stanza?

The meaning of "The Lord possessed me" (8:22) is "I was the Lord's." (See Notes.) Do the verses teach that the Lord's wisdom is from eternity?
4. *Stanza 8:32-36.* Compare this stanza with 8:1-11. Which is your favorite verse of 8:32-36?

---

5. *Stanza 9:1-12.* Mark verses 7-9 in your Bible as a parenthesis. This will help you see the continuity of thought from 9:1-6 to 9:10-12. What is the point of the description of verses 1-3?

What is the woman's invitation (9:4-6) and instruction (9:10-12)?

Of the former, compare Isaiah 55:1; John 6:35; Revelation 22:17. Also, compare the great supper of Luke 14:16-24. What is the point of the parenthesis (9:7-9)?

---

6. *Stanza 9:13-18.* What spiritual lessons about evil do you learn from these verses?

III. NOTES

1. *"The Lord possessed me"* (8:22). In some versions the word "possessed" is "made" or "created." The phrase "I was brought forth" (8:24-25) is then translated as "I was born." The weakness of these translations is that the divine attribute of wisdom is taught as having a beginning, thus not eternal. An accurate paraphrase of

44

8:22*a* would be, "I, Wisdom, was the Lord's in the beginning; yea, I was with Him from all eternity." Those who see Christ pictured throughout chapter 8 must be careful in their interpretation of the text lest the *eternal* being of Christ is contradicted.

2. *"The highest part of the dust of the world"* (8:26). A correct translation is "the first dust of the world." (Cf. Gen. 2:7.)

3. *"Seven pillars"* (9:1). The number *seven* may have a symbolic intention. Seven is the number of perfection, and the suggestion here may be that Wisdom is fully prepared to satisfy.[1]

4. *"Knowledge of the holy"* (9:10). The intention is personal: "knowledge of the Holy One."

5. *"Stolen waters"* (9:17). "Whereas Wisdom offers a feast indeed and of her own preparation (5), Folly offers a paltry meal, stolen, illicit and clandestine (17), and her guests go to their death (18)."[2]

6. *"Hell"* (9:18). The Hebrew word is *sheol*, the name for the place of departed souls in Old Testament times. The compartment of sheol for unbelievers was one of torment; for the believer it was a place of bliss (cf. Luke 16:19-31). All thirty-one appearances of the word "hell" in the King James Version's Old Testament translate *sheol*. At the last judgment, the great white throne judgment of Revelation 20:11-15, all unbelievers will be cast into the lake of fire for eternity. This place of endless judgment is what is usually meant by the word *hell*.

IV. FOR THOUGHT AND DISCUSSION

Apply chapters 8-9 to Christians. Is it true that two choices face believers constantly: the choice to obey Christ's Word and the choice to disobey it? What have you learned from your study of this lesson that will help you to be faithful to Christ?

V. FURTHER STUDY

With the help of a Bible dictionary and concordance, study the Bible's use of the three words "hades," "sheol," and "hell." Related subjects will be suggested by a Bible dictionary.[3]

1. R. Laird Harris, *The Wycliffe Bible Commentary*, p. 565.
2. W. Jones and A. Walls, "Proverbs," in *The New Bible Commentary*, p. 526.
3. Three recommended Bible dictionaries are J. D. Douglas, ed., *The New Bible Dictionary* (Grand Rapids: Eerdmans, 1960); Merrill F. Unger, *The New Unger's Bible Dictionary*; and Merrill C. Tenney, ed., *The Zondervan Pictorial Bible Dictionary*. Two recommended concordances are James Strong, *The Exhaustive Concordance of the Bible* (New York: Abingdon, 1890); and Robert Young, *Analytical Concordance to the Bible* (Grand Rapids: Eerdmans, n.d.).

VI. WORDS TO PONDER

Her guests are in the depths of hell (9:18*b*).

"The end is the wormwood and the gall, when the anguished soul, bowed in bitterness that shall never be alleviated forever, is forced at last to confess how dreadful has been the mistake of turning from the call of Wisdom to seek the deceitful allurements of Folly."[4]

---

4. H. A. Ironside, *Notes on the Book of Proverbs*, pp. 91-92.

Lesson 7

Marks of Godly Living

Until now Proverbs has identified who the truly wise man is. From this point on it will describe how such a man should conduct his life from day to day. This logical topical order appears in many New Testament epistles, where the saved person is first identified and then the daily life he should live is described. Two examples from Paul's writings illustrate this:

Rom. 1-5: the condemnation of the sinner and how he may be saved
6-8: how to live the Christian life
Eph. 1-3: the believer's heritage in Christ
4-6: the believer's walk in Christ

Our study of Proverbs 1-9 has shown that the truly wise man is the one who fears the Lord and commits his life to Him by faith. In Old Testament times a good example of a saved man was Abraham, of whom it was said, "He believed in the Lord; and he [the Lord] counted it to him [Abraham] for righteousness" (Gen. 15:6; cf. Rom. 4:3). One earmark of a believer is that he wants to please God by his life. How may he know what pleases his heavenly Father? The indwelling Holy Spirit reveals this to him, primarily through the Scriptures, which He inspired. That is why such a large proportion of the Bible is addressed to believers, to show them how they should think, speak, and act.

It is true that many, if not most, of the practical maxims of Proverbs 10-31 can be applied to all people everywhere. But these chapters were written primarily for the benefit of believers, those who in chapters 1-9 are identified as the "wise" ones. Do you want to please your Lord by how you *live* as a Christian? Proverbs 10-31 will give you the Lord's standards, and it may surprise you that He is interested even in the details of your personal life.

47

I. PREPARATION FOR STUDY

1. Now that you are about to begin studying a new section of Proverbs, it will profit you to review the survey Chart C, to recall things studied in Lesson 2. Note the following on that chart:

(a) The section 10:1–22:16 is made up mostly of one-verse maxims. They are identified in 10:1 as "The proverbs of Solomon." There are 184 maxims in chapters 10-15, and 191 in chapters 16-22, totaling 375.[1] At 22:17 longer and more general proverbs begin to appear.

(b) Most of the proverbs of chapters 10-15 are *antithetic*, using the key word "but" (e.g., 10:1). In chapters 16-22 there are more *synonymous* maxims, using the key word "and" (e.g., 16:6).

(c) The proverbs of 10:1–22:16 are mainly observations of Solomon as he viewed life under the inspiration of the Spirit. Beginning at 22:17 commands and exhortations appear, putting to practice the maxims of the preceding chapters.

2. Do not try to complete this lesson in one sitting, since the Bible passage involved is long (6 chaps.). When you begin to analyze parts of chapters, you can decide how much to study at one time. It is important to guard your study from becoming superficial.

3. Read Psalm 1 for a good commentary of Proverbs 10-22. As you begin your study of this lesson, answer the following question, and ponder the implications of it: Why is the word *but* a repeated word throughout the Bible?

II. ANALYSIS

Passage to be analyzed: 10:1–15:33
Stanza divisions: (see the work sheets)

It is difficult to detect *groups* of maxims in this section. The present chapter divisions in the Bible may have been made mainly on the basis of length (averaging around thirty verses per chapter). Some expositors maintain that all the proverbs of this section are detached from each other, constituting one long miscellaneous list. F. Delitzsch takes the position that the editor (arranger) of the proverbs "did not throw them together by good chance, but in placing them together was guided by certain reasons."[2] J. A. Bengel's experience was this: "I have often been in such an attitude of soul, that those chapters in the Book of Proverbs in which I had

---

1. According to 1 Kings 4:32, Solomon was the author of 3,000 proverbs.
2. F. Delitzsch, *Proverbs of Solomon*, 1:208.

before looked for no connection whatever, presented themselves to me as if the proverbs belonged in the most beautiful order one with another."[3] I believe that even though groups of proverbs in these chapters are usually not obvious as far as common subject is involved, the Bible student will deepen and broaden his analysis if he approaches the text with the purpose of finding connections between individual proverbs that Solomon or an arranger may have had in mind. Later in this lesson some possible groupings of proverbs will be suggested as a basis for your individual study. You may want to look for groupings yourself. If you do, mark such groups in your Bible and study these units as you analyzed stanzas in the earlier lessons.

Work Sheet Analysis

The work sheets shown in the following pages have three main functions:
1. to show possible locations of topical divisions
2. to suggest topical outlines following those decisions
3. to provide space for you to record your own observations of content
As you read the chapters verse by verse, refer to the outlines, and try to identify the Bible phrases on which the outlines are based. (Note: Every proverb located in a particular group need not specifically refer to the subject shown in the outline.) Then devote time to arriving at your own conclusions as to outlines, isolated thoughts, and so forth. Record your studies in the spaces provided. You may want to record only key or favorite proverbs in each stanza.
Chapters 13-14 are one long list of proverbs contrasting the righteous man and the ungodly man. On paper mark off four columns, and record what each proverb says about any of the following subjects: Righteous Man Described, Good Fruits; Ungodly Man Described, Evil Fruits. (Note: Because so many proverbs are involved in these two chapters, you may want to record observations only on selected ones.)
Chapter 15 says much about the tongue, the spoken word, and the heart. Read the chapter and underline in your Bible every reference to this subject. Derive some practical lessons from your study.

3. Quoted in John Peter Lange, "Proverbs," in *Commentary of the Holy Scriptures*, p. 33.

OUTLINES	PASSAGE	OBSERVATIONS, OUTLINES, OR FAVORITE PROVERBS
THINGS IN LIFE THAT PROFIT	10:1-14	
Righteousness	1	
Diligence	4	
Obedience	6	
Love	11	
LIFE AT ITS BEST	10:15-32	
Its Course	15	
Its Outreach to Others	18	
Its Fruits	22	
RIGHTEOUSNESS WORKS EVERYWHERE	11:1-15	
In Business	1	
In Personal Problems	5	
In Government	9	
SURE REWARDS	11:16-31	
For Christian Virtues	16	
For Liberal Giving	24	
For Seeking Good	27	

THE ROOT OF THE RIGHTEOUS	12:1-12	
Unmovable	1	
Pure	4	
Fruitful	9	
A STUDY OF CONTRASTS	12:13-28	
Prudent Lips	13	
Slothful Heart	24	
Conclusion	28	

III. NOTES

1. Some words of the King James Version are rendered more clearly in other versions. Here are two examples from the *New American Standard Bible:*
10:23, "mischief": "wickedness" (NASB)
10:31, "froward": "perverted" (NASB)
2. *"He that winneth souls is wise"* (11:30). The first line of this verse helps to explain this phrase. "The fruit of the righteous is a tree of life." A Christian by his example and witness attracts others to give their hearts to Christ, so that his righteousness is a tree of life to others.

IV. FOR THOUGHT AND DISCUSSION

1. What does the Bible teach about material wealth? Compare 10:15 and 18:11. What is the sin of such a rich man?
2. Read 11:24-29. In what different ways have you experienced the blessing of giving to others?
3. Read these verses about women: 11:16; 11:22; 12:4; 14:1. Compare the descriptions with those made in the earlier chapters: 2:16; 6:24, 26, 32; 7:5, 10; 9:13. How vital is the woman's role in the

course of the human race? What are your thoughts about the saying "The hand that rocks the cradle rules the world"?

4. What are some of your favorite proverbs of chapters 10-15? If you are studying in a group, share with each other your favorites.

V. FURTHER STUDY

The immortality of the soul is a teaching of 12:28. This doctrine appears often in the New Testament. Read the following Old Testament references to immortality: Job 19:25-27; Psalm 16:10; 17:15; Isaiah 25:8; 26:19; Ezekiel 37:10; Daniel 12:2. Why would a person prefer to believe in the annihilation of the soul after death?

VI. WORDS TO PONDER

When a good man speaks, he is worth listening to, but the words of fools are a dime a dozen (10:20, TLB).

Reverence for God adds hours to each day; so how can the wicked expect a long, good life? (10:27, TLB).

The backslider gets bored with himself; the godly man's life is exciting (14:14, TLB).

A relaxed attitude lengthens a man's life; jealousy rots it away (14:30, TLB).

Ways of Man That Please the Lord

The next seven chapters continue the practical theme of chapters 10-15, but the style is different. Whereas the earlier proverbs were mainly antithetic, using the key word "but," now they are primarily the parallel type, using the word "and." The purpose of the former is to emphasize by contrast; in the latter it is to emphasize by repetition and addition. Here is a proverb in the opening verses of this lesson: "By mercy and truth iniquity is purged: and by the fear of the Lord men depart from evil" (16:6). We shall be studying in this lesson many of the ways of man that please the Lord (16:7).

I. PREPARATION FOR STUDY

1. Review the opening pages of the last lesson, since much of what was written there applies to this lesson as well.

2. Refer to Chart C again, noting the context of the passage of this lesson.

3. Always keep in mind as you study these proverbs that they are not mere secular maxims recorded for the benefit of society. More than that, these proverbs were included in the Book of God to show His redeemed people how to live godly lives. Paul wrote to Titus that Christians should "live soberly, righteously, and godly, in this present world," and by so doing they would "adorn the doctrine of God our Saviour in all things" (Titus 2:12 and 10). Who knows but that Paul often referred to Proverbs whenever he and his fellow believers studied the Scriptures?

II. ANALYSIS

Passage to be analyzed: 16:1–22:16
Segment divisions: at the beginning of each chapter

Study this passage chapter by chapter, using the suggestions given below as a guide for your analysis. As you complete each chapter, mark in your Bible those proverbs that appear outstanding.

A. 16:1-33: Trusting the Lord as Sovereign King of the World[1]

This chapter breaks down into the following groups:

> 16:1-9 — The Lord
> 16:10-15 — Kings
> 16:16-31 — Miscellaneous Proverbs
> 16:32 — Kings
> 16:33 — The Lord

MAIN SUBJECTS OF 16:1—22:16   **Chart K**

chap.	16	17	18	19	20	21	22
heart	1-2						
speech	13						
walk							
Lord							
judgment							
wisdom							
evil							
possessions							

1. Some of the titles assigned to the chapters of this lesson are adapted from Lange's commentary.

Read 16:1-9, underlining the repeated phrase "the Lord" in your Bible. (See Notes.) How is the Lord shown to be sovereign over the whole world?

_____

_____

Read 16:10-15. Note the repeated word "king." What is the main theme of these verses?

_____

_____

Observe the concluding two verses of the chapter. Is the subject of kings implied in verse 32? Note how the last verse teaches the sovereignty of the Lord.

Chart K is a work sheet to record verse references about the subjects listed. Read chapter 16 verse by verse, and record the number of each verse in the appropriate column. (Examples are shown.) This will help you grasp the varied content of this chapter and the ones that follow. You may want to add subjects to the list. (Note that the first three categories are about thought, word, and deed, respectively.)

B. 17:1-28: Peacemakers and Troublemakers

Mark this three-part outline in your Bible:

17:1	Theme
17:2-9	Contrasts Mainly as to Speech
17:10-20	Contrasts Mainly as to Deeds
17:21-28	Wisdom and Folly Contrasted

What contrasts are introduced in verse 1?

_____

_____

Read the entire chapter, recording on Chart K the main subjects that appear. Note all the references to speech in 17:2-9. Note the many references to strife in 17:10-20. Read what James wrote about strife in James 3:13–4:12. Also observe what is taught about wisdom and folly (godliness and ungodliness) in the last stanza.

C. 18:1-24: How to Be a Good Neighbor

Interspersed among the varied maxims of this chapter are references to a person's relations with other people. Read the chapter, and observe those references. Make a list of spiritual lessons to be learned from them.

D. 19:1–22:16: Miscellaneous Maxims

These chapters contain more than one hundred miscellaneous maxims. There is no detectable grouping of proverbs under any one subject. If you record the verse references of main subjects on Chart K, you will observe that while the proverbs are scattered as to subject, each proverb can be classified under one of the chart's eight subjects. Here is a list of selected proverbs from these chapters. After you have read each one, record your reflections.

19:6

_____

19:11

_____

19:17

_____

19:18

_____

20:6

_____

20:11

_____

20:12

_____

20:29

_____

21:17

_____

21:23

_____

22:1

_____

22:6

_____

III. NOTES

1. *"The Lord"* (16:1). The name "Lord" (Jehovah) appears eighty-six times in the book. Thirty-four of those references are in the passage of this lesson. It is good to be reminded that the Lord is the key to all righteous living, as its Author, Standard, Inspirer, Empowerer, Judge, and Rewarder.

2. *"Having separated himself"* (18:1). The Bible speaks of two kinds of separation. "To separate from apostasy is right and scriptural. To separate from what is of God is schism and heresy."[2] Most commentators interpret the separatist of 18:1 as a schismatic, selfish individualist, breaking fellowship with other people. Harris takes another view, that "the separated is the one wrongfully separated from God, seeking his own desire, not the Lord's."[3]

3. *"The spirit of man is the candle of the Lord"* (20:27). Man was made in the image of God (Gen. 1:27). The deepest, eternal part of man is his spirit. (Cf. Zech. 12:1; 1 Cor. 2:11.) This distinguishes him from animals. Man is conscious of God through his spirit, and he hears God's voice through his spirit. In this sense his spirit is the candle, or lamp, that holds and thus receives the light revealed from God. Man's spirit is "imponderable—it cannot be weighed; intangible—it cannot be handled; invisible—it cannot be seen."[4]

IV. FOR THOUGHT AND DISCUSSION

1. Illustrate the truth of 16:25 from Bible stories or from everyday life in the world today.

2. Compare 17:17 and 18:24b. How is Jesus the perfect Friend? See John 13:1 for one description of His love.

3. Read Titus 2:14. For what two reasons did Christ die? How does the phrase "zealous of good works" reflect what should be the Christian's attitude toward the book of Proverbs?

4. The name "God" appears only eight times in Proverbs, whereas the name "Lord" ("Jehovah") appears eighty-six times. One writer has observed that "the name 'Jehovah' belongs especially to Him when He is dealing with His own, while 'God' is used more when dealing with the Gentiles . . . for instance 2 Chronicles 18:31."[5] If this explains the one-sided proportion noted

---

2. H.A. Ironside, *Notes on Proverbs*, p. 227.
3. R. Laird Harris, "Proverbs," in *The Wycliffe Bible Commentary*, p. 571.
4. Herbert Lockyer, *All the Doctrines of the Bible* (Grand Rapids: Zondervan, 1964), p. 144.
5. Arthur B. Fowler, "Jehovah," in *The Zondervan Pictorial Bible Dictionary*, ed. Merrill C. Tenney, p. 408.

above, to whom is Proverbs mainly addressed: the believer or unbeliever?

5. What does the book of Proverbs have to do with the lordship of Christ in the life of a believer? See Luke 6:46.

V. FURTHER STUDY

Study what the Bible teaches about "conscience," using such aids as a book of doctrines, a word study book, and an exhaustive concordance.

VI. WORDS TO PONDER

The horse is prepared against the day of battle: but safety is of the Lord (21:31).

Lesson 9

Proverbs 22:17–24:34

Applying God's Word to Our Living

The main feature of this lesson's passage is the constant appeal to apply the instruction received. The key phrase "apply thine heart" appears in the opening verse (22:17) and is repeated at 23:12. At only one other place does the word "apply" appear in the book (at 2:2). We observed in the earlier lessons that the 375 short maxims of 10:1–22:16 were mainly statements of truth describing godly and ungodly living. They were the observations and reflections of Solomon. Now beginning at 22:17 the emphasis is on application: determining in the heart to walk righteously, in line with the proverbs already given. Ironside comments:

> Many have been the words of wisdom to which we have been listening; many more are to follow. The soul may become so used to them as to fail to discern their excellent character. *What is needed is that the heart be applied to the knowledge thus imparted.* For it is of all importance that they be kept within and fitted to the lips of the hearer . . . if he is to exemplify them in his life.[1]

I. PREPARATION FOR STUDY

1. Read the concluding appeal that Solomon wrote in Ecclesiastes 12:13. How are the commands reflected in the common phrase "trust and obey"? How does the verse summarize the purpose of the book of Proverbs?

2. Read Luke 6:43-45. What is taught here about a man's deeds? How does the book of Proverbs relate to this?

3. Look at Chart C again, and note that the word "observation" identifies the section 10:1–22:16, and the words "exhorta-

---

1. H. A. Ironside, *Notes on Proverbs*, p. 310. Emphasis supplied.

tion" and "warning" identify 22:17–24:34. How else is this latter section identified?

4. Recall how frequently the phrase "My son" appeared in the first nine chapters (fifteen times). In the long section of 10:1–22:16 the phrase did not appear at all, because the purpose of those chapters was description, not appeal. Now, beginning at 22:17, the author returns to that personal father-son contact and gives warm counsel by way of exhortation and command. Someone has aptly said that at 22:17 "the reader feels a hand on his shoulder again."

II. ANALYSIS

Passage to be analyzed: 22:17–24:34
Stanza divisions: at verses 22:17, 22; 23:12, 26; 24:1, 23, 30

A. General Analysis

Chart L shows an outline of the general contents of this passage. Use the blank spaces for recording some of your observations as you proceed with your study.

COUNSEL OF WISE MEN 22:17—24:34   **Chart L**

INTRODUCTION — 22:17
WHAT TO AVOID — 22:22
WHAT TO EMBRACE — 23:12
SNARES OF EVIL WOMEN — 23:26
WISDOM AND FOLLY — 24:1
PROVERBS — 24:23
PARABLE — 24:30
MORE WORDS OF THE WISE — 24:34

Scan briefly the Bible text of each stanza, and note the following:

1. The first stanza introduces the whole section. Note the phrase "the words of the wise" (22:17).
2. Read 24:23. Compare this verse with 22:17. Because of the word "also," the section 24:23-34 is sometimes referred to as an appendix or supplement.
3. Note the repeated negatives in the text of 22:22–23:11 (hence the title "What to Avoid"). Then note how the next stanza (23:12-25) emphasizes the positive ("What to Embrace").

B. Stanza Analysis

1. *Introduction: 22:17-21.* The phrase "the wise" (v. 17) is plural and could be translated "the wise men." Who do you think is meant by this?

_____

Is it possible that some of the proverbs of this section (e.g., 23:26ff.) could have originated with Solomon? (Cf. 1 Kings 4:29-34; Prov. 1:6; Eccles. 12:9, 11.)
What different things are said in this introductory stanza about the instruction of Proverbs?

_____

_____

2. *What to avoid: 22:22–23:11.* Using your own words, make a list of don'ts for Christians, based on these verses. For help on some phrases, compare the readings of a modern paraphrase, for example, *The Living Bible.* Note how many commands are followed by reasons for obeying the command.
3. *What to embrace: 23:12-25.* How much of this stanza is about parent-child relationships?

_____

What commands are given?

_____

_____

4. *Two snares: 23:26-35.* What are the two snares of this passage?

_____

_____

How are they related to each other?

_____

5. *Wisdom and folly: 24:1-22.* Here is the familiar dual theme of Proverbs again. Note how often wisdom is spoken of in the first half of the stanza and wickedness in the last half. What are some of the major teachings here?

6. *More words of the wise men: 24:23-34.* State in your own words the meaning of each of the proverbs of verses 23-29. What is the one main teaching of the parable of verses 30-34 (cf. 6:6-11)?

III. NOTES

1. *"Excellent things"* (22:20). Some translate this as "thirty things," that is, thirty proverbs.[2]

2. *"Be not thou one of them that strike hands"* (22:26). Here is an interesting paraphrase of this verse by *The Living Bible*: "Unless you have the extra cash on hand, don't countersign a note. Why risk everything you own? They'll even take your bed!"

3. *"Their redeemer is mighty"* (23:11). Christ's work as Redeemer is a key doctrine of the New Testament. It relates basically to man's bondage to sin. In Christ "we have redemption through his blood, the forgiveness of sins, according to the riches of his grace" (Eph. 1:7). Through Christ's blood (the ransom) a sinner is delivered from the enslavement of sin and released to a new freedom. A glance at an exhaustive concordance shows the title "redeemer" appearing often in the bright messianic chapters of Isaiah 40-66.

4. *"Wine"* (23:31). As noted in lesson 4, the Hebrew has two words for wine. In this verse (and in 23:20) it is *yayin*, which means fermented wine. The other word is *tirosh*, which in 3:10 refers to the fresh product of the pressing, or grape juice.[3]

5. *"Every man shall kiss his lips"* (24:26). This obscure verse has been interpreted in different ways, as suggested by the following translations or paraphrases:

"He kisses the lips who gives a right answer" (NASB).

"The right word spoken seals all, like a kiss on the lips" (Knox).

"It is an honor to receive a frank reply" (TLB).

"He that equippeth his lips [i.e., with wisdom] shall give a right answer" (*New Bible Commentary*).

2. Refer to a commentary for a discussion of this phrase.
3. R. Laird Harris, "Proverbs," in *The Wycliffe Bible Commentary*, p. 560.

IV. FOR THOUGHT AND DISCUSSION

1. What are the associated evils of slothfulness (24:30-34)? How can a Christian employee be a good witness for Christ to his employer by how he performs at his job?

2. The advice "Count the cost first, then build" can be applied to many aspects of our lives. (Cf. Luke 14:25-33; Prov. 24:27.) What has been your experience concerning this?

3. Do you think the law of just recompense applies to everybody, believers as well as unbelievers? Read Proverbs 24:12; Matthew 16:27; Hebrews 2:1-4. Does the element of time play a part in the execution of divine justice?

4. Does God help orphans and poor people today? (See 22:22-23; 23:10-11.) If so, how?

5. What causes some people to hold that man cannot know truth? Observe the phrase of 22:21 "know the certainty of the words of truth." Read 1 John 5:13-20, and observe the repeated word "know." Is assurance of salvation a vital ingredient of that salvation?

V. FURTHER STUDY

1. Study the Bible's use of the word "redeemer" (and its cognates, e.g., "redemption"). Read articles on "redemption" in such books as a Bible dictionary.

2. Some commentaries point out likenesses between Proverbs 22:17–23:12 and the Egyptian writing *Wisdom of Amen-em-Opet*. You may want to inquire into this.

VI. WORDS TO PONDER

Buy truth, and do not sell it (23:23a, NASB).

Lesson 10

Further Descriptions of Godliness

These chapters contain proverbs that Hezekiah's staff collected 250 years after Solomon wrote them. We learn from 1 Kings 4:32 that Solomon authored 3,000 proverbs. Of that number, the ones that God decreed and inspired to be part of Holy Scripture eventually were brought together into the one book Proverbs. The details of how this book became a unit are not given by the Bible, partly because such details are not determinative in one's study of the Bible text. The fact of Hezekiah's part in this collecting was deemed worthy of note, hence the reference in the opening verse of 25:1.

The entire Hezekiah section (chaps. 25-29) is a series of miscellaneous proverbs describing the godly ("wise") man. Chart M shows that the descriptions of chapters 25-26 are mainly comparative, whereas the descriptions of chapters 28-29 are made mainly by contrasts, using the word "but." This is mentioned again later in the lesson.

GENERAL STYLES OF CHAPTERS 25-29   **Chart M**

chap. 25	26	27	28	29
MAINLY COMPARISONS			**MAINLY CONTRASTS**	
"as . . . so"		COMPARATIVE AND ANTITHETICAL	**"but"**	

I. PREPARATION FOR STUDY

Chart N shows the kingships of Solomon and Hezekiah in relation to each other. Solomon was the last king before the kingdom was split (resulting in the Northern Kingdom of Israel and the Southern Kingdom of Judah). During Hezekiah's reign over Judah, Israel was taken into captivity by the Assyrians (722 B.C.). There was an interval of 250 years between Solomon and Hezekiah (c. 950-700 B.C.).

Hezekiah was one of Judah's greatest kings. The reforms and revival in Judah under his leadership are suggested by these verses: "So the service of the house of the Lord was set in order" (2 Chron. 29:35). "So there was great joy in Jerusalem: for since the time of Solomon the son of David king of Israel there was not the like in Jerusalem" (2 Chron. 30:26). "And thus did Hezekiah throughout all Judah, and wrought that which was good and right and truth before the Lord his God. And in every work that he began in the service of the house of God, and in the law, and in the commandments, to seek his God, he did it with all his heart, and prospered" (2 Chron. 31:20-21). (Read the following passages for further descriptions of Hezekiah's ministry: 2 Kings 18-20; 2 Chron. 29-32; Isa. 36-39.) At some time during his reign Hezekiah commissioned a group of men to compile the proverbs of Solomon that are now identified as chapters 25-29 (25:1). Why do you think Hezekiah would encourage his people to read and study such proverbs? If the proverbs were important then, are they less important now?

II. ANALYSIS

Passage to be analyzed: 25:1–26:28

A. General Analysis

Scan the two chapters, and observe the variety of subjects covered by the maxims. Note the repeated use of "as . . . so" in the proverbs beginning at 25:11. This figure of speech is called a *simile*. What are some of its teaching values? Did Jesus like to illustrate spiritual truths by observable things and events of everyday life?

B. Stanza Analysis

1. *Opening: 25:1-10.* The reference to Hezekiah as "king of Judah" (25:1) anticipates the various references to kings (and other

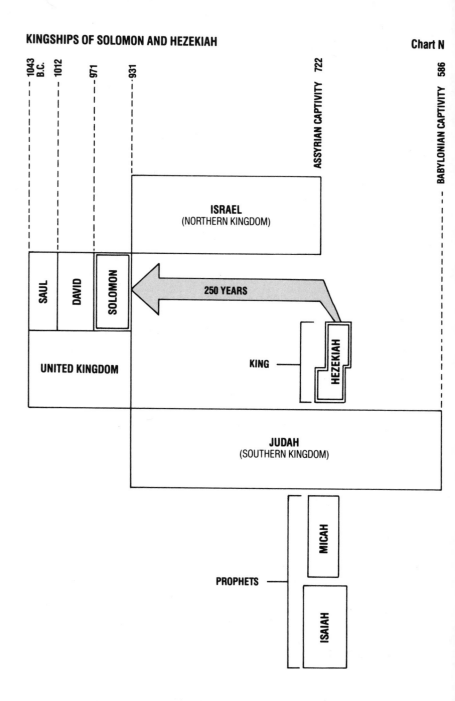

rulers) in the next verses. Underline these in your Bible in verses
2-7. What is said about kings in verses 2-5?

_____

_____

What is the advice of these next two parts:
25:6-7

_____

25:8-10

_____

2. *Similes: 25:11–26:28.* As noted earlier, most of the proverbs of
this section are of the comparative type. At first glance it appears
that each maxim stands by itself in one long miscellaneous list. Actually, many of the proverbs have been arranged in groups of
common content, as suggested in the study exercises that follow.[1]
(a) *Speech* (5:11-15). What different kinds of oral communication
are mentioned here?

_____

What are the practical lessons?

_____

(b) *Overindulgence* (25:16-17). Apply the principle of verse 16 to
situations not involving food. Compare verse 17 with the saying
"Familiarity breeds contempt."
(c) *Enmity* (25:18-19). What two kinds of enmity are mentioned
here?

_____

(d) *Sympathy* (25:20-22). What is the implication of verse 20?

_____

Compare Romans 12:20-21 with Proverbs 25:21-22.

_____

(e) *Miscellaneous maxims* (25:23-28). Here are some interesting
and important bits of advice about everyday living. (See Notes on

1. This arranging into groups was one of the tasks of Hezekiah's compilers.

67

v. 23.) Try to reconstruct situations involving Christians today where these proverbs would apply. Compare Proverbs 25:24 with Ephesians 5:22-24.

(f) *The fool* (26:1-12). The main theme of this cluster of proverbs is suggested by the repeated word "fool." Underline in your Bible every appearance of the word. In your own words, what is the theme? Recall from earlier studies who is represented in the spiritual realm by the "fool" of Proverbs. In the words of Ironside, "Fools are those who make a mock at sin, rejoicing in iniquity, and refusing to heed the voice of wisdom."[2]

To learn the meaning of these proverbs in the spiritual realm, it will help to first study each proverb for its literal meaning in a secular context. Read the proverbs one by one. Determine what each one means in everyday life, without reference to unbelievers only. For example, verse 3 teaches the necessity of correction and chastisement, to keep a person from persisting in his foolish ways. Regarding the figurative meaning in the spiritual realm, go back over the proverbs and apply each one to the life of an unbeliever. For example, verse 12 teaches that a sinner who admits his unsaved state is closer to the kingdom of God than a self-righteous egotist who claims he is one of God's children.

(g) *The sluggard* (26:13-16). The sin of folly of the previous verses (26:1-12) is the underlying sin of unbelief and rejection of God. Beginning with the next group of verses (26:13-16), the sins are those that may be found in the life of a Christian, sins that Christians should repent of and confess. Apply 26:13-16 and the following groups with this in mind. For example, why should Christians not be found guilty of sloth?

(h) *The meddler* (26:17). How does "yanking a dog by its ears" illustrate the ways of a busybody?

(i) *The practical joker* (26:18-19). Read the question, "Am not I in sport?" as, "Was I not joking?" (NASB).

(j) *The gossip* (26:20-22). How destructive is gossiping in the Christian church?

---

2. H. A. Ironside, *Notes on Proverbs*, p. 361.

(k) *The hypocrite* (26:23-28). What proverbs in this group are specifically about hypocrisy and deceit?

III. NOTES

1. *"Men of Hezekiah"* (25:1). These may have been scribes who were assigned to the literary department of Hezekiah's kingdom. Some scholars think there was a royal library in Jerusalem at this time similar to ones in Babylon and Assyria:

> The most striking feature of Assyrian and Babylonian culture was the libraries, where scribes were kept constantly employed, not only in writing and compiling new books, but in copying and re-editing older ones. The 'men of Hezekiah' who 'copied out' the proverbs of Solomon performed duties exactly similar to the royal scribes in Nineveh.[3]

2. *"Copied out"* (25:1). Opinion is divided as to whether the Hebrew word means collected, edited, or recopied. (Compare various versions.) It is possible that the men of Hezekiah performed all three services.

3. *"God to conceal... kings... to search out"* (25:2). Paul wrote this of God's secrets: "O the depth of the riches both of the wisdom and knowledge of God! How unsearchable are his judgments, and his ways past finding out!" (Rom. 11:33). Because God is God, He rightly does not share all things with His creatures. "But though He so acts, He would have those in authority (e.g., the kings of 25:2) search earnestly His word that they may find out His mind and will."[4]

4. *"Pictures of silver"* (25:11). The *New American Standard Bible* and Berkeley Version translate this as "settings of silver." Some paraphrase the word "pictures" as "basket" (TLB). The meaning of the simile is the same for both readings.

5. *"Vinegar upon nitre"* (25:20). Nitre was equivalent to our soda and was found in the alkali lakes of Egypt. When an acid like vinegar was combined with nitre, the effect was active foaming. The picture is one of disturbance or violence. A person who acts frivolously and lightheartedly toward one in deep distress will only agitate his condition. See Ecclesiastes 3:4.

3. Prof. Sayce, quoted by T. T. Perowner, in *The Proverbs* (Cambridge: U. Press, 1916), p. 156.
4. Ironside, p. 345.

6. *"The north wind driveth away rain"* (25:23). A common weather pattern in the Northern Hemisphere is the passage of a cold front through an area. Just ahead of the front the weather is relatively warm and rainy, with southerly winds. With the passing of the front the weather changes to cooler and clearing, with northerly winds. Note how each of these two different weather conditions supports one or the other of the following translations of 25:23:

> The north wind driveth away rain: so doth an angry countenance a backbiting tongue (KJV*; cf. TLB).
> The north wind brings forth rain, and a backbiting[5] tongue, an angry countenance (NASB; cf. Berkeley).

Compare the meanings of the second lines. Which translation do you prefer?

7. *"As the bird by wandering"* (26:2). Ironside comments on the subject of false accusation suggested in this proverb: "As the sparrow and swallow cleave the air and pass quickly from view, so shall it be with a curse uttered without cause."[6]

8. *"The great God that formed all things"* (26:10). Note by the italics in your Bible that the word "God" is not in the Bible manuscripts. All translators are agreed that the meaning of this verse is difficult to determine because various translations of the Hebrew words are possible. See the text and marginal note of the *New American Standard Bible* for two alternate readings.

IV. FOR THOUGHT AND DISCUSSION

1. If you are studying in a group, discuss these three aspects of Christian living:
(a) Humility: What examples has Christ given us?
(b) The tongue: Read James 3.
(c) Work: Read 2 Timothy 2:15 (NASB).
2. *"Love covereth all sins"* (10:12*a*). Apply this truth to the different sins mentioned in the proverbs of this lesson.

V. FURTHER STUDY

Make a comparative study of the topic of slothfulness as this appears in the Bible. Here are suggested passages to read: Proverbs

---

*King James Version.
5. The word tanslated "backbiting" means literally secret, or concealed, which implies talking behind one's back (cf. Berkeley).
6. Ironside, p. 362.

6:6-11; 10:4-5; 12:24, 27; 13:4; 15:19; 18:9; 19:15, 24; 20:4; 21:25; 23:21: 24:30-34; 26:13-16; Ecclesiastes 10:18; Isaiah 56:10; Matthew 25:26-27; Romans 12:11; 2 Thessalonians 3:10-12; Hebrews 6:12. With the help of a concordance read also verses about idleness (e.g., 1 Tim. 5:13).

VI. WORDS TO PONDER

If a godly man compromises with the wicked, it is like polluting a fountain or muddying a spring (25:26, TLB).

Lesson 11
Good and Evil

Proverbs 27:1–29:27

Our study of this lesson continues in the proverbs of Solomon, which were compiled by Hezekiah's aides. For the most part the maxims of these chapters are antithetical, contrasting righteous conduct and evil ways. The prominent word is "but," especially in chapters 28 and 29. This is shown on the outline of Chart O.

CHAPTERS 25-29 COMPARED **Chart O**

CHAPTERS	TYPES	EXAMPLES
25 26	MAINLY COMPARISONS "as . . . so"	An example: "AS coals are to burning coals, and wood to fire, SO is a contentious man to kindle strife" (26:21).
27	A mixture of comparisons and contrasts	
28 29	MAINLY CONTRASTS "but"	An example: "The rod and reproof give wisdom: BUT a child left to himself bringeth his mother to shame" (29:15).

I. PREPARATION FOR STUDY

Before you read the proverbs of this lesson, think about the principles suggested in the following questions, and give your own answers:

72

Do you think outward deeds in the life of a Christian (e.g., contributions to poor people) are as important as exercise of the heart (e.g., confession of sin to God)?

Are these two kinds of expression related, and, if so, what does this imply? (Note: The two examples cited above are taken from two proverbs of this passage. Read 28:27 and 28:13.)

II. ANALYSIS

Passage to be analyzed: 27:1–29:27

A. Methods of Analysis

Except for 27:23-27, there are no topical groupings of proverbs in these chapters. Occasionally you will observe two adjacent verses treating the same subject, but these do not represent substantial *groups* as such. It is correct to say that this passage is a miscellaneous collection of detached proverbs. One way to study the maxims is to proceed verse by verse as in a devotional study, noting the spiritual truths being taught and applying them accordingly. For this lesson we will follow a topical approach, studying scattered proverbs that have been brought together under specific topics. (Note: Since the total passage is a lengthy one, divide your work into at least three study units. If you are studying with a class, your group leader should determine how long each unit should be.)

B. Topical Analysis

Read each proverb listed in a particular group. Record on paper in your own words the lesson being taught by each maxim. (Sometimes only one line of the maxim applies to the subject.) After you have finished reading each whole group, compare the different proverbs.[1]

1. *Evil ways*
   (a) Pride and self-sufficiency: 27:1, 2, 7, 21 (TLB); 28:11, 14, 25-26; 29:1,23
   (b) Deceit: 27:5-6, 14, 19 (TLB); 28:13, 23; 29:5, 12, 13
   (c) Folly-wickedness: 27:22; 28:5, 12, 28; 29:2, 6, 9, 11, 16, 20, 24 (TLB), 27
   (d) Oppression of others: 28:3, 8, 10, 15-17, 24; 29:10
   (e) Wrath: 27:3-4; 29:8, 20, 22
   (f) Purposelessness and irresponsibility: 27:8, 13; 28:1; 29:18

---

1. Every proverb of 27:1–29:27 appears in at least one group of this listing.

(g) Envy: 27:4, 20
(h) Greed: 28:20, 22
(i) Disobedience to God's law: 28:4, 9
(j) Evil women: 27:15-16; 29:3
(k) Partiality: 28:21
2. *Righteous ways*
    (a) Fear of God: 28:14, 18, 20, 25; 29:25
    (b) Wisdom-righteousness: 27:11, 12; 28:5, 12, 26; 29:2, 3, 6, 9, 11, 16, 27
    (c) Faithfulness to others: 27:10 (TLB), 18; 28:20; 29:14
    (d) Friendly counsel: 27:9, 17; 28:23; 29:15, 17, 19, 21
    (e) Stewardship: 27:18, 23-27; 28:18
    (f) Obedience to God's law: 28:7; 29:18
    (g) Justice: 29:4, 14, 26
    (h) Unselfishness: 28:27
3. *Two other subjects*
    The proverbs listed below could be classified under "evil ways," or "righteous ways," or under both.
    (a) Government: 28:2; 29:2, 4, 12, 14, 26
    (b) Poverty: 28:6, 11; 29:7, 13, 14

III. NOTES

1. *"Transgression of a land"* (28:2). This proverb was pertinent in Hezekiah's day because he saw the Northern Kingdom of Israel taken into captivity (722 B.C.) for their sins. (See Chart N.)
2. *"Where there is no vision"* (29:28). The Hebrew word translated "vision" refers to the visionary experience of a man of God receiving revelation from God. (Read Ps. 89:19; Isa. 1:12; and Jer. 14:14, where the same word appears.) The second line of the verse, with its reference to the law of God, supports this meaning. "Where the revealed will of God, as expressed in His Word, is not kept constantly in view, His people break loose from their allegiance."[2]

IV. FOR THOUGHT AND DISCUSSION

The variety of areas of living represented by these proverbs suggests that a Christian's faith involves his total life. Do you recall what Jesus taught that verifies this?

2. W. Jones and Andrew Walls, "The Proverbs," in *The New Bible Commentary*, p. 536.

V. FURTHER STUDY

Jesus preached the Sermon on the Mount to describe the kind of life that Christians—citizens of His Kingdom—should be living. Read Matthew 5-7, and compare the teachings with some of the proverbs of this lesson.

VI. WORDS TO PONDER

Where there is ignorance of God, the people run wild; but what a wonderful thing it is for a nation to know and keep his laws! (29:18, TLB).

Lesson 12
The Words of Agur

The last two chapters of proverbs are an epilogue, added by the compiler to the maxims of Solomon. Chapter 30 is identified as "the words of Agur" (30:1), and chapter 31 as "the words of king Lemuel" (31:1). Although their style differs from Solomon's writings for the most part, their practical counsel about righteous living blends with the rest of the book.

This lesson is about "the words of Agur." You will find the chapter to be an interesting one, partly because of the change of style. Always keep in mind as you study that "all Scripture is given by inspiration of God, and is profitable for doctrine, for reproof, for correction, for instruction in righteousness: that the man of God may be perfect, throughly furnished unto all good works" (2 Tim. 3:16-17).

I. PREPARATION FOR STUDY

1. Review the survey Chart C, observing how these last two chapters are associated with the preceding ones.

2. Read the opening title of 30:1. What four names appear here? Consult a Bible dictionary for an identification of each name.

This verse can be translated in different ways, depending on whether the original Hebrew word is transliterated as a proper name or translated with a meaning.[1] Here are some possibilities:

(a) "the prophecy": "of Massa"[2]; of "the burden"[3]

---

1. Most Hebrew names have a meaning. E.g., Jacob means "supplanter." See R. Laird Harris, "Proverbs," in *The Wycliffe Bible Commentary*, p. 580.
2. The Hebrew word is *massa*. Cf. Gen. 25:14.
3. The word "massa" is translated "burden" in such verses as Isa. 13:1; 15:1.

(b) "unto Ithiel, even unto Ithiel and Ucal": "I have wearied myself, O God, I have wearied myself, O God, and I languish."

3. This chapter is made up mostly of numerical proverbs. A numerical proverb is one that is introduced by a number reference, for example, "There be four things" (30:24). In chapter 30 four poems are introduced by the unique combination "There are three things . . . yea, four" (e.g. 30:15). The purpose of such a device may be simply to indicate that the list is not exhaustive, though specific. Or the purpose may be to emphasize the fourth item of the list. Harris points out that this climactic method was also used by Jesus in the Beatitudes.[4] Read Matthew 5:3-6 and 5:7-10, and observe the distinctive fourth item in each instance.

II. ANALYSIS

Segment to be analyzed: 30:1-33
Stanza divisions: at verses 1, 5, 7, 10, 11, 15, 17, 18, 21, 24, 29, 32

A. General Analysis

After you have marked the stanza divisions in your Bible, read through the chapter for first impressions. Compare the humble testimony of 30:2-3 with the reference to pride in the last stanza.

B. Stanza Analysis

All the stanzas of this chapter are short. The practical truths are timely, incisive bits of wisdom. Spend a lot of time here. Extend your studies beyond the few questions given below.

1. *Longing for the knowledge of God: 30:2-4.* What do verses 2 and 3 reveal about Agur? (Note the emphasis on the pronoun "I.")

Are the questions of verse 4, or similar ones, asked by people today? Compare the prominent pronoun of this verse with that of verses 2 and 3. Read Job 38:4-41; John 3:13; Ephesians 4:9-10; Romans 10:6-10. What comes to mind when you read the phrase "his son's name" (v.4)?

Read Colossians 1:16-17 for Christ's part in the work of creation.

4. Harris, p. 581.

2. *God's Word: 30:5-6.* What do these verses teach about God's Word?

_____

3. *Two requests: 30:7-9.* What are the two things desired by Agur?

_____

What temptation may accompany riches?

_____

What temptation may accompany poverty?

_____

4. *Relation to others: 30:10.* Compare Romans 14:4 with this command.

_____

5. *Four detestable things: 30:11-14.* What sins are exposed here?

_____

_____

6. *Four insatiable things: 30:15-16.* What spiritual lessons do you learn from these verses?

_____

_____

7. *Relation to others: 30:17.* Compare this verse with 30:11.

_____

_____

8. *Four inscrutable things: 30:18-20.* See Notes on the word "wonderful." How is the fourth item, "the way of a man with a maid," the prominent one of this numerical proverb?

_____

Do you think the description of the adulteress in verse 20 refers to the same situation just recorded: "the way of a man with a maid"? Or do you think this is an entirely different observation of Agur?

_____

9. *Four intolerable things: 30:21-23.* Consult a modern version for the reading of these verses. What common problem do these four situations bring on?

_____

_____

10. *Four things little and wise: 30:29-31.* This is a favorite proverb of the Bible. What is the main point?

11. *Four stately things: 30:29-31.* See Notes on verse 31. What should a Christian's posture and bearing be as far as his spiritual life is concerned?

12. *A concluding admonition: 30:32-33.* What sins are mentioned here?

How are these verses a fitting conclusion to the entire chapter?

III. NOTES

1. *"Knowledge of the holy"* (30:3). The writer's intention is personal: "knowledge of the Holy One" (NASB).
2. *"Horseleach"* (30:15). This parasite is a blood-sucking worm. It is a fitting description of a creature "never satisfied" (30:15).
3. *"Wonderful"* (30:18). The Hebrew word has the connotation of something distinguished. It is used in the Bible in connection with either good or bad things. For an example of the latter, read Deuteronomy 28:59. In 2 Chronicles 2:9 the word describes a good thing.
4. *"The way of a man with a maid"* (30:19). The word translated "maid" is *almah*, meaning "virgin." (See Isa. 7:14; Gen. 24:43.) Some interpret the phrase to describe sinful enticement.[5] Harris comments: "There seems to be no good reason why the more romantic view cannot still be held: Wonderful is the way of courtship, issuing at last in the mysteries of love and life begotten."[6]
5. *"Odious woman"* (30:23). Some versions translate this as "unloved woman" (see NASB), which is a more literal rendering of the Hebrew text.
6. *"Spider"* (30:28). The first line of this verse is accurately translated "The lizard you may grasp with the hands" (NASB). Two verses in the Bible about spiders are Job 8:14 and Isaiah 59:5.

5. See H. A. Ironside, *Notes on Proverbs*, p. 449.
6. Harris, p. 581.

7. *"Greyhound"* (30:31). The meaning of the Hebrew is unclear. The Berkeley Version translates this as "fighting cock."

8. *"A king, against whom there is no rising up"* (30:31). Various translations of this line are:

   (a) "a king when his army is with him" (NASB)
   (b) "the king accompanied by his army" (Berkeley)
   (c) "a king as he leads his army" (TLB)
   (d) "the king speaking publicly before his nation" (Greek Septuagint)

IV. FOR THOUGHT AND DISCUSSION

1. What are some of the good practical lessons taught in this chapter that can be applied to Christian living? For example, what can be learned from the ants?

2. One of the most profound utterance in the Bible is "knowledge of the Holy One" (30:3, NASB; cf. 9:10). What do you think is meant by this phrase? How may one have such a knowledge? Ponder the following words of A. W. Tozer in his book *The Knowledge of the Holy*:

> The words, "Be still, and know that I am God," mean next to nothing to the self-confident, bustling worshiper in this middle period of the twentieth century.
>
> Modern Christianity is simply not producing the kind of Christian who can appreciate or experience the life in the Spirit.
>
> We have lost our spirit of worship and our ability to withdraw inwardly to meet God in adoring silence.
>
> The low view of God . . . is the cause of a hundred lesser evils everywhere among us.[7]

V. FURTHER STUDY

"Every word of God is pure" (Prov. 30:5). God's Word is God's communication to man of Himself. The glad tidings of salvation are a prominent part of that Word. Read the following different references to that redemptive Word, as they appear in various New Testament books:

"word of God" (2 Cor. 2:17; 4:2)
"word of the Lord" (Acts 15:36)
"word of his grace" (Acts 14:3)
"word of the cross" (1 Cor. 1:18, NASB)
"word of the truth" (2 Cor. 6:7)

7. A. W. Tozer, *The Knowledge of the Holy* (New York: Harper & Row, 1961), p. 5.

"word of the gospel" (Acts 15:7)
"word of the truth of the gospel" (Col. 1:5)
"word of this salvation" (Acts 13:26)
"word of reconciliation" (2 Cor. 5:19)
"word of life" (Phil. 2:16)
"word of righteousness" (Heb. 5:13)
"word of faith" (Rom. 10:8)
"word of Christ" (Rom. 10:17, NASB)

VI. WORDS TO PONDER

If you have been foolish in exalting yourself ... put your hand on your mouth (30:32, NASB).

Lesson 13

Proverbs 31:1-31

The Words of Lemuel

Proverbs's final chapter is of two parts: counsel to a king and praise of a righteous woman. The chapter is attributed to Lemuel (31:1), who quotes his mother's counsel in 31:10-31. It is appropriate that Proverbs concludes with instruction about two of the largest institutions of the human race: the nation and the home.

I. PREPARATION FOR STUDY

You may want to consult a commentary for various views on who Lemuel was (31:1). The main point of the opening verse is clear: a mother gave the counsel of verses 2-9 to her son, who was a king.

II. ANALYSIS

Segment to be analyzed: 31:1-31
Stanza divisions: at verses 1, 2, 10

A. Counsel to a King: 31:2-9

Note the many references to kings and rulers in this stanza. What are the different kinds of advice given to the king?

_____

_____

B. Praise of a Good Woman: 31:10-31

1. This is an acrostic, or alphabetical, poem. Its twenty-two verses in the original Hebrew begin with the successive letters of the He-

brew alphabet. (Similar acrostics: Ps. 119; Lam. 1) Read the stanza with this outline in mind:
 (a) a good woman sought (31:10)
 (b) a good woman described (31:28-31)
 (c) a good woman praised (31:28-31)
Which line of the entire stanza do you believe is the secret of this woman's praiseworthiness?

2. Make a topical study of this passage using the title and outline given below.[1] Fill in each blank with an appropriate description (an example is given).

MRS. "FAR-ABOVE-RUBIES"

She is a good woman

vv. 13, 15, 19:   She works diligently.

v. 16 (also vv. 22, 24:   She _____

v. 25:   She _____

She is a good wife

v. 12:   She _____

v. 11:   She _____

vv. 23-24:   She _____

She is a good mother

v. 21:   She _____

vv. 15, 27:   She _____

vv. 14, 18:   She _____

She is a good neighbor

v. 20*a*:   She _____

v. 20*b*:   She _____

v. 26:   She _____

1. Title and outline are from J. Sidlow Baxter, *Explore the Book* (Grand Rapids: Zondervan, 1960), 3:139.

III. NOTES

1. *"Give strong drink unto him"* (31:6). H. A. Ironside writes of this:

> There is a tinge of undisguised irony in the sixth and seventh verses. . . . Strong drink might help the despondent to forget their poverty and to remember their misery no more; but the true remedy is for the judge of the oppressed to hear their cause patiently and render a decision in righteousness, as he cannot do if under the power of wine.[2]

2. *"Virtuous woman"* (31:10). The same phrase appears at 12:4. A literal translation is "noble wife." The *New American Standard Bible* reads "excellent wife."

IV. FOR THOUGHT AND DISCUSSION

Since this is the last lesson of your study of Proverbs, it will be helpful to think over the entire book and try to recall its major teachings. Answer the following questions briefly and concisely on the basis of Proverbs:

1. What is the righteous life?
2. What is the life of folly?
3. What place do good works have in the life of a Christian?
4. "You reap what you sow" (cf. Gal 6:7). Does this apply to Christians? If so, how and when?
5. How is Christian living related to the glory of God?

V. CONCLUSION

The heart attitude that brings a sinner back into fellowship with God is that of faith, trust, and godly fear. This truth underlies the multitude of maxims about works and deeds that appear in the book of Proverbs. A key phrase of Proverbs that represents this is "the fear of the Lord." Recall that the title given to the book on Chart C is "Walking in the Fear of the Lord." The Christian who truly fears and knows the Lord will grow in spiritual stature day by day so that his conduct will reflect more and more the exhortations of this inspired book.

Three verses of Proverbs including the phrase "the fear of the Lord" represent the span of Christian life from conversion to glory. (Note the progression, chapterwise):

2. H. A. Ironside, *Notes on Proverbs*, pp. 471-72.

1. First chapter: "The fear of the Lord is the BEGINNING of knowledge" (1:7).
2. An intervening chapter: "Be thou in the fear of the Lord ALL THE DAY LONG" (23:17).
3. Last chapter: "A woman that feareth the Lord. . . . Give her of THE FRUIT of her hands" (31:30-31; eternal rewards suggested).

May your study of Proverbs have given you a clearer vision of "that good, and acceptable, and perfect, will of God," and with it a dedication of your whole being as "a living sacrifice, holy, acceptable unto God" (Rom. 12:1-2).

Appendix
Familiar Proverbs

Below is a list of some of the more familiar proverbs. Read each proverb, and record its main point. Do some of them remind you of other parts of the Bible? Perhaps you have experienced the truth of some in a personal way.

1:7

3:13

4:23

11:30

14:9

15:3

15:31

16:3

16:11

16:18

16:28

16:28

16:31

18:4

18:10

18:22

20:1

20:15

22:1

22:6

22:28

23:23

23:31-32

25:11

25:25

26:8

27:1

28:19

Bibliography

COMMENTARIES AND TOPICAL STUDIES

Aiken, Kenneth T. *Proverbs*. Philadelphia: Westminster, 1981.
Arno, William. *Studies in Proverbs*. Grand Rapids: Kregel, 1978.
Bridges, Charles. *An Exposition of Proverbs*. Evansville: Sovereign Grace Book Club, 1959.
Delitzsch, F. *Proverbs of Solomon*. Vols. 1 and 2. Grand Rapids: Eerdmans, 1950.
Harris, R. Laird. "Proverbs." In *The Wycliffe Bible Commentary*, ed. Charles F. Pfeiffer and Everett F. Harrison. Chicago: Moody, 1962.
Ironside, H. A. *Notes on the Book of Proverbs*. New York: Loizeauz, n.d.
Jones, W., and Walls, Andrew. "The Proverbs." In *The New Bible Commentary*, ed. F. Davidson. Grand Rapids: Eerdmans, 1953.
Kidner, Derek. *The Proverbs*. Downer's Grove, Ill: InterVarsity, 1964.
Phillips, John. *Exploring the Scriptures*. Chicago: Moody, 1965.
Zockler, Otto. *Commentary on the Holy Scriptures, Proverbs*. Edited by John Peter Lange. Grand Rapids: Zondervan, n.d.

RESOURCES FOR FURTHER STUDY

Archer, Gleason L. *A Survey of Old Testament Introduction*. Chicago: Moody, 1964.
Jensen, Irving L. *How to Profit from Bible Reading*. Chicago: Moody, 1985.
_____. *Jensen's Survey of the Old Testament*. Chicago: Moody, 1978.

Manley, G. T. *The New Bible Handbook*. Chicago: InterVarsity, 1947.

Mears, Henrietta C. *What the Bible Is All About*. Glendale, Calif.: Gospel Light, 1953.

New International Version Study Bible. Grand Rapids: Zondervan, 1985.

New Scofield Reference Bible. New York: Oxford, 1967.

Pfeiffer, Charles F.; Rea, John; and Vos, Howard F.; eds. *Wycliffe Bible Encyclopedia*. Vols 1 and 2. Chicago: Moody, 1975.

The Ryrie Study Bible. Chicago: Moody, 1985.

Strong, James. *The Exhaustive Concordance of the Bible*. New York: Abingdon, 1890.

Tenney, Merrill C., ed. *The Zondervan Pictorial Bible Dictionary*. Grand Rapids: Zondervan, 1963.

Unger, Merrill F. *The New Unger's Bible Dictionary*. Chicago: Moody, 1988.

Moody Press, a ministry of the Moody Bible Institute,
is designed for education, evangelization, and edification.
If we may assist you in knowing more about Christ
and the Christian life, please write us without obligation:
Moody Press, c/o MLM, Chicago, Illinois 60610.